Gene Olson was born in Bothell, WA.

He was sent to Vietnam as a part on Navy and spent time on ships in Mekong Delta and Saigon River.

He was diagnosed with bipolar illness after returning from Vietnam and struggled with the illness for the rest of his life although always remained himself.

He married a girl from Poland who was a physician and helped him a lot with his struggles.

They have two beautiful sons and a grandson.

This is a story of survival, courage and honesty in our imperfect world.

For my beautiful wife, Jolanta.
God sent this angel from Poland to Seattle just in time.

Gene Ellis Olson

# BIPOLAR BOY FROM BOTHELL

AUSTIN MACAULEY PUBLISHERS™

LONDON • CAMBRIDGE • NEW YORK • SHARJAH

**Ordering Information**
Quantity sales: Special discounts are available on quantity purchases by corporations, associations, and others. For details, contact the publisher at the address below.

**Publisher's Cataloging-in-Publication data**
Olson, Gene Ellis
Bipolar Boy from Bothell

ISBN 9781649794291 (Paperback)
ISBN 9781649794307 (ePub e-book)
ISBN 9781649794284 (Audiobook)

Library of Congress Control Number: 2022923336

www.austinmacauley.com/us

First Published 2023
Austin Macauley Publishers LLC
40 Wall Street, 33rd Floor, Suite 3302
New York, NY 10005
USA

mail-usa@austinmacauley.com
+1 (646) 5125767

In memory of my parents:

George Olson
1915–91
My father, my dad, the Swede
Loved me unconditionally.

Violet Mortenson Olson
1918–2008
My mother, my mom, the Norwegian
Loved me more than I knew.

This world was not their home.
They were just passing through.

# Table of Contents

Biography and Autobiography/General     11

Prologue     12

Chapter 1: A Time to Be Born     13

Chapter 2: First Recollections     15

Chapter 3: Mini-Farm Adventures     19

Chapter 4: Starting School – Learning to Learn     26

Chapter 5: Bothell Senior High School – Fun and Friends     38

Chapter 6: Church and God     49

Chapter 7: A Change in Course     54

Chapter 8: The President Sends a Letter     62

Chapter 9: Navy Boot Camp     65

Chapter 10: Ship is Found     73

Chapter 11: Okinawa and Office of Naval Intelligence (ONI)     85

Chapter 12: Leave/Liberty     95

Chapter 13: Final Cruise     99

Chapter 14: College Bound Again     103

Suicide in Seattle     155

The Blue Room     157

The Angels Never Came     158

The Cross from the Boys Home     161

Chapter 15: Seeds of Manic Depression Germinate     162

Chapter 16: Return to the Pancake House     170

Chapter 17: Vietnam and Rich     172

Chapter 18: Fairfax Psychiatric Hospital     175

Chapter 19: Seattle Veterans Administration Medical Center     180

Chapter 20: Coping with Thorazine     185

Chapter 21: American Lake     190

Chapter 22: Searching for Self-Sufficiency     202

Chapter 23: My Angel from Poland     210

Chapter 24: Second Honeymoon – Polish Style     217

Chapter 25: Together Again, Finally     228

Chapter 26: Becoming a Hoosier     241

Chapter 27: It's Vancouver, Washington, not
                Vancouver, British Columbia     249

Epilogue     264

# Biography and Autobiography/General

It has been written that you should not write memories unless you are famous, an actor, or have unusual experiences. The author is not famous. He is not an actor. But his life has been filled with many unusual experiences.

After dropping out of college in 1965, the escalation of Vietnam caught the author. Army released him to the navy. Amphibious Force, Saigon River, and Mekong Delta, a lot different from the Pacific Northwest. Then Okinawa would be the place of an investigation with ONI, the Office of Naval Intelligence.

How or when bipolar seeds started sprouting is still a mystery. Walk with the author in his first psychiatric hospital, then years in and out on the Seattle VA Hospital Psych Ward. Finally, during the summer of Bicentennial of '76 at America Lake VA Medical Center in Tacoma, Washington, after five months, God healed his mind with lithium.

*The Bipolar Boy from Bothell* is the author's fight for sanity.

And how God never left his side.

Gene lived most of his life in the Pacific Northwest. He has traveled extensively in Europe. He currently resides in Vancouver, Washington, with his wife.

And two adult sons out of the nest.

# Prologue

I have a manic-depressive illness or "bipolar disorder." The disease has no cure, some say—but there is hope. After six years of searching, I found lithium. My bipolar family is extensive and growing rapidly each year.

Bipolar disorder (also known as manic-depressive illness) affects nearly six million adults in the United States. This psychiatric disorder was first described at the time of Hippocrates and is currently one of the most prevalent and severe mental illnesses in our society (Consultant, January 2008, Vol. 48, No. 1).

Psychiatry and pharmaceutical research have traveled supersonic speed in developing and understanding better treatments for the mentally ill. Research still continues, but the road is long. People are still suffering, still wondering, still lost in anguish, still needlessly dying in confusion.

I am the Bipolar Boy from Bothell. Bothell, Washington, sits on the northeast corner of Lake Washington. Follow the lake along Bothell Way NE and after a few miles, you're in Seattle city limits.

The paths through the woods, the gravel roads for my bike, the highway for my first car—a 1955 red and white Chevy—the friends and memories of Bothell will never depart. I left Bothell, but I will always be *The Bipolar Boy from Bothell*. The beginning paths were smooth and sunny. Then the storms came. College. South Vietnam. Bipolar disorder.

Throughout the years, I never wanted to die. I wanted to live! The fight was great! The Author of Confusion lost.

My steps begin where life begins—at birth.

# Chapter 1
# A Time to Be Born

The year 1945 was one to remember. The first bumper stickers appeared on cars. Fluoridated water and frozen orange juice invaded American kitchens. The zoom lens made picture-taking more than "snapshots." And Tupperware gave housewives a reason to save leftovers.

Bud Abbott and Lou Costello made a movie in 1945 called *The Naughty Nineties*. A segment, *Who's on First*, continues to be a classic comedy routine today.

John W. Mauchly and J. Presper Eckert unveiled the electronic computer ENIAC (Electronic Numerical Integrator and Computer). The birth of computers was ignited.

But the greatest historical event in 1945 was the end of World War II and the beginning of the Nuclear Age. Germany formally surrendered on 7 May. After atomic bombs destroyed Hiroshima on 6 August and Nagasaki on 9 August, Japan surrendered. Adolf Hitler committed suicide. And it was hard to understand and believe the film footage coming out of Eastern Europe—concentration camps run by Lucifer himself and his devils—cremation, experiments, sexual exploitations, starvation, gas, and death.

As news spread "THE WAR IS OVER!" celebrations started from the East Coast to the West Coast. Cheers and dancing in the streets left everyone euphoric. "The war to end all wars" was finally over.

In the fall of 1945, Seattle, like the rest of the nation, was basking in peace. The future ahead lay shining bright with dreams and plans for a better tomorrow.

12 October 1945, 3:20 a.m., the peace and calm in Seattle were briefly interrupted. With a mighty cry, I entered the world at Doctors' Hospital as Gene Ellis Olson. The fourth child of a Norwegian mother and a Swedish father...a mixed Viking, ready for the world.

Mother claims she took castor oil so I would be born on Columbus Day. She wanted a Columbus Baby. She received her wish—but minus eyelashes.

The event could not compare to "THE WAR IS OVER," but I was happy to start living. I was ready to go. Too young to dream, too young to plan, but not too young to smile and cry. Not too young to drink and poop, but just right to be a baby.

The world was ahead of me. The journey down many roads had just begun.

# Chapter 2
## First Recollections

Memory travels great distances—and so does my mind. Perhaps the earliest recollection, though fuzzy, happened in the master bedroom. I can't visualize the house, but I do see a bedroom, dimly lit. I'm lying on my mom's stomach, near her breasts, seeing, touching, cuddling. I don't remember being hungry or thirsty. I don't remember sucking her breasts.

I have no recollection of the house on Burke Street, north of Seattle, close to the University of Washington, only a photograph.

At seventeen days old, I won a prize for being the youngest baby in church at Seattle First Church of the Nazarene. I only remember because of a mother's pride. The first visit was the beginning of many to come.

When I was just eleven months old, the family moved across Lake Washington to Bellevue. In the late forties, the east side of Lake Washington was simply the "east side of Seattle." Not much developing, only the small growing towns of Bellevue Kirkland, and Bothell. No Microsoft, no Seattle Seahawks football headquarters.

Five acres, a little red brick house, country, country—this was home for three years. It was my first taste of acreage, animals, nature, and open space.

A little after we moved, Mother brought home from the hospital a thin baby sister. I was instantly her eleven-month-older brother. Mother said when I first saw her, I poked my finger in her eye. I don't remember the poke, but I remember in the coming years proclaiming, "No, we're not twins! I am eleven months older!"

In Bellevue, I cherished my little red plastic piggy bank. Every penny I found or was given went directly into "piggy." I was to save pennies and not open it. But a time came when the bank could hold no more pennies.

I had to figure out how to open "piggy." I tried and tried, but nothing, no pennies. Mother was sitting at the kitchen table with a neighbor drinking coffee; this was my chance. Now I quietly sneaked by the kitchen table with the piggy bank in one hand and a very large, heavy hammer in the other. Outside, I placed everything on the sidewalk. Raising the hammer as far up over my head as possible, POW! The smashed little piggy bank flew into a thousand pieces. All the pennies rolled and scattered in every direction. Poor little piggy bank!

I quickly gathered all the pennies; both hands were full, bulging. The thought came, *If I can just get back into the house without getting caught.*

With hands hidden in back to hide the evidence, I walked slowly, cautiously past the kitchen. I almost made it…

"What do you have in the back of your hands?" Mother asked sharply.

Being a child about to be caught for the first time and lacking experience in "bank smashing," I replied with the only answer I knew, "Nothing!"

"Show me your hands."

That was it. I was caught! With pennies bulging and slipping from each hand, I had no choice but to surrender.

As I held both hands outstretched, the pennies once again went flying and rolling. I was caught!

I learned a valuable lesson. "If you do something wrong behind the back, eventually you will be caught in the front."

Soon another valuable lesson would be learned.

Being so small, I never left the property unless accompanied by a member of the family.

Once I went with my father to a nearby woods. He was going to dig some wild ferns to transplant into our yard. The main road passing our house and woods was small gravel. Since the road was elevated from the woods, I stayed on the shoulder as my father dug ferns below.

The inviting small rocks of the gravel underfoot were too tempting for a toddler to resist. Not only could I throw one rock but with a handful, I could throw many rocks at the same time.

Few cars traveled this road. Then one appeared. The car appeared closer and closer. I picked up the biggest fist full of gravel I could manage.

"Ready. Aim. Throw. Yes! Splattered the side, good! But wait a minute. Why is the car stopping? Why is the car moving backwards toward me?"

A tall man (all men were tall) stepped out of the car, walked over, and gave me a spanking. I was surprised!

"Don't ever do that again!" he warned and drove off.

I never did it again.

My son was a little bigger, almost preschool, when a huge rock was inviting to him. Too bad it wasn't small gravel. A dog was barking four houses down. He picked up a rock with the intention of hitting the dog to stop it from barking so loud. However, the rock was so big and his arm so small. Consequently, instead of flying four houses down, it fell short in the neighbor's front yard. And in the neighbor's front yard was parked a new Corvette. On the outside of the Corvette was a power mirror...

Well, it used to be a nice power mirror.

Later in the day, the neighbor asked, "Do you know anything about my smashed mirror?"

I wanted so much to say "no," but I couldn't. I had seen it all. A spanking for my son would have been easier than paying the three-hundred-dollar repair bill!

My little, little sister was soon walking around. Though we'd be mistaken for twins many times in the near future, in a sense we were twins. From the beginning of her life, she taught me what a lady was, what femininity meant in its truest form, and that there was a vast difference between boys and girls. Her lessons were precious.

No one knows who "instigated" the "let's go play in the car" episode. I remember my version.

The family station wagon was an old "Woody" DeSoto. Dark brown, carriage rack on top and the classy wood on the sides made our car special. Soon our fascination at playtime ended up on the front seat. The dashboard with all the gadgets and numbers put me in a delighted state. And the steering wheel, so smooth and easy to turn!

The station wagon was parked on a slight incline, facing left of the garage below. Standing on the front seat with both hands gripping the large steering wheel, I convinced my little sister to release the emergency brake. Slowly, slowly, the car rolled forward, picking up speed. I was driving! CRASH! My steering needed improvement.

The left side of the garage door was the casualty. More trouble ahead.

My sister and I still debate: who was the steeree and who was the brakee?

Sunday afternoon drives were always exciting. It meant going places, seeing things never before seen. It was never in the city, always in the country.

At the time I didn't know it, but Mom and Dad were actually scouting for a new home.

The best part of the drive was the end, stopping in Lake City for soft ice cream cones. I was convinced Mom was trying to steal some of MY ice cream when she licked the dripping edges. Convinced...until I had children.

Countryside drives ended after several months. Mom and Dad had discovered property they loved. It was about a mile from a small town called Bothell; five acres with a big, old gray house perched on a hill. There were also a barn and smaller buildings. It was still on the east side of Lake Washington, but farther north from Bellevue and Kirkland.

This mini-farm was a "plantation" for me to discover.

The Olson Family was moving to Route 1, Box 12, Bothell, Washington. At four years old, I was moving from childhood to boyhood. The year was 1949.

# Chapter 3
# Mini-Farm Adventures

Bothell is my hometown. I say it with pride. I say it with affection. Though born in Seattle, Bothell is the place where I grew up and out. Going from kindergarten through high school in the same school district develops deep friendships, friendships growing each year.

But as a preschooler, I had plenty of time to explore our new mini-farm

To the north of our property lived Chris Rotegard. In the thirties, he had home-steaded about ten acres of land and built a small one-bedroom house and two large barns.

The first-time visiting Chris, I came home and told Mom all the "new" words I had learned. It didn't take Mom long to send the word to Chris. "If you swear in front of our Gene, he cannot visit you again." He never swore in front of me again.

Excitement was a small word to express my feelings when I was invited to Chris's for breakfast. It was only me!

The musky smell, darkness, and everything old, yes, old, this was where Chris lived. He was stocking the wood stove, first with small pieces, then larger one. I noticed in the side of the stove a hot streak of flame burning fast. Chris told me he had fixed a line from outside to an oil barrel to give better burning power.

As Chris was loading the fire, I thought for sure the flames would jump out and there would be fire, fire everywhere. But no.

It was time for breakfast. He mixed the pancake batter. But where was the pan? There was no pan. He just poured the mix right on top of the stove!

"Now, watch closely," Chris said. "When you start seeing bubbles on the top, it's time to turn them over."

Sure enough, before long bubbles did appear. Bubbles all over! And that's the last thing I remember about breakfast with Chris.

Months later, as I grew older, I would spend many hours with Chris on his homestead. He would be a grandfather I never knew.

A favorite time to play was on the long road reaching to our house on the hill.

The banks cut sharp and left soft dirt ready for my imagination. I had no cars at first. But many rocks and stones looked just like cars. I made roads, some straight, some curvy, fun for the cars to travel.

I wanted to taste the dirt. But I found as I bit down, the tiny rocks were too hard to chew. Dirt was not good to eat!

Meeting my first big black ant was a surprise. He first appeared on my hand while I was playing in the dirt. I watched him closely. He started climbing my index finger which I held pointing up. He was big! He climbed and climbed around my finger. Reaching the top, he raised up his hind legs, came down and pinched me on the tip of my finger. Just when I was beginning to like this little ant!

My little sister played a lot with me. She didn't like the dirt. But that was OK. I'm not sure who was to blame for the "Match Party." Oh, it had to be my little sister.

Mom was resting in the bedroom. My little sister slyly talked me into quietly sliding a chair over to the cupboard and "borrowing" a bunch of big wooden matchsticks. She would be the "lookout" in case Mom woke up. And I think it was her alibi, "I didn't take the matches," in case we were caught.

The woods were the best place to play since no one could see us. With matches clutched in hand, we raced to the big rock. This rock was bigger than a big rock! I struck the first matchstick; it broke in half. I tried again. A burst of flame startled me, burning a little finger. I threw the match down. It landed on a nearby old dried-up evergreen bough—POOF! Flames surrounded everywhere! We ran. We ran fast! Was the forest on fire? Did we start a forest fire? Playing with matches—luckily, no forest fire.

Growing older, I realized we lived on a mini-farm with cows, calves, chickens, and rabbits. Nothing felt like a calf sucking on your fingers…slimy with pressure. Just put out your hand and they came, sucking, sucking, leaving your hand slippery.

Milking the cow was assigned to Dad. This was important and could not be taken lightly. The family needed milk. Every chance I could get, I was following, watching being near Dad. This was true at milking time. How fascinating to see milk coming from those "things" dangling down! One morning I was completely engrossed milking process, but getting too close. Since I was getting in the way, Dad asked to step back. Several minutes passed. My foot seemed warmer. I glanced down. In the center of the milk bucket was my foot! Time to strain the milk again!

I loved playing with the rabbits! We would let them out of their little cages to come play and eat fresh clover. They would never run away, just jump a little, content to have some freedom. So cute and furry.

My father was a butcher. He didn't butcher anyone. He just butchered animals. I

was glad when he became a meat cutter. That sounded a lot better.

I could hardly watch as my dad "skinned" and "butchered," yes butchered, my rabbit friends. He did it like a professional. But I was mad. How could d do it?

Sad news came at dinner—rabbit was on the menu! I was not hungry I could not eat my friends!

The first walk in the deep woods was scary. Being the smallest and shortest, I usually ended up at the end of the line. As we walked into the woods, suddenly giant plants sprang up on each side of the path. On the stem and branches were long prickly needles; needles like Mom used to sew—only longer! And there were so many, millions!

George, my older brother, warned us, "Be very careful. If one of those needles touches your skin, it will go into your bloodstream, straight to your heart and you will die instantly!"

Wow! I wasn't going to touch anything! The name itself brought fear—'Devil's Clubs.'

My older brother, Glenn, a few years older, had the distinction of giving me a nickname. Mom was calling me into the house, "Gene, Gene!" \Glenn was also calling, "Geehoney, Geehonny!"

"Isn't that cute?" Mom said. "He's saying Johnny." From then on, I was nicknamed "Johnny."

Mom had a project. She bought all the used coats from the Salvation on Army, Goodwill, and other thrift stores. This was the beginning of the Rug of Ma y Colors. She cut the coats into narrow strips. The children would roll the separate colors into balls. This was not easy. Once I rolled a big ball, it got away and I had to start all over.

From the rolls, Mom sewed the pieces together with a carpet needle to make long strands. Then the braiding started. I didn't know how to braid. The braids ere sewn together in a circle. What a colorful rug! Within days, the wood floor was completely covered by the Rug of Many Colors. And now we had a place for afternoon naps.

A delight as a child was receiving my very own transistor radio—"Made in Japan." It even had a small plastic earpiece for private listening. Just a few stations, but I only needed one. This was the birth of my love for music.

The transistor radio momentarily lost its appeal when Dad brought home a small black-and-white television. What commotion in the house on the hill! The first program I saw was a silent western. A group of cowboys kept hitting and pushing men into a well.

My favorite show was about a jungle boy always riding an elephant, always a tiger on the run and yes, those fierce scorpions; it was frightening! The commercial focused on children's shoes.

"Hi, I'm Buster Brown. Look for me. I'm in the shoe."

The camera would zoom in on the shoe with his picture inside. Make no mistake, Buster Brown Shoes wanted to sell only true Buster Brown Shoes.

The comedy of Laurel and Hardy made me laugh and still does today. There was no doubt Davy Crockett was "King of the Wild Frontier." Just ask any kid, myself included, about the coonskin cap he was wearing.

Out of the night when the full moon is bright. Zorro captivated me. Just how could he make that "Z" on everybody and everything? And he did it so fast!

No one likes rejection. It hurts the most, especially the first time in boyhood. The day before my birthday things were happening without me included. Everyone was heading to Chris's property. "Sorry, Gene, you cannot come with us," my older brother George said with no explanation.

And why? Why couldn't I come?

Feeling low and left out, I walked up a small hill to the corner of the woods that bordered Chris's property. It was isolated, a great hiding place, but you could still see the house and pasture through the trees. I would retreat to this wonderful place many times in the future. Sometimes to play. Sometimes to cry. Other times to think.

Looking down at the blacksmith shop, I could see figures moving. But what were they doing? Why couldn't I be there? It wasn't fair!

Next day my birthday came. My brothers rolled out a brand-new fire-engineered wagon they had assembled in secret, the best birthday present I had ever received. Yesterday was forgotten.

I rolled down the hill in back of the blacksmith shop. It was a fast wagon! Two older boys asked if they could try it. They jumped on like they were snow sledding. The wagon picked up speed. At the bottom of the hill, "CRACK," the front axle broke. My birthday present was busted!

The older I became, the more visits I made to our neighbor Chris. His little one-bedroom house was always a favorite place. And the bedroom was haunting, dark. But one picture on the wall caught my interest—the picture of a girl, a beautiful girl, sitting under tree branches on a rock by the ocean. She had no clothes on. I stated. Her hair was long, blond and curly, and covered some of her breasts. She sat with her right leg bent halfway up and resting her body with her arms.

Chris also had chickens, cows, and horses. He never penned the chickens, just let them run free. Once there was a lot of commotion in the Barnyard. A chicken hawk was circling the barn. Chris became angry, went into the house, and came back out with a 22-gauge rifle. No bird was going to eat his chickens! He fired several shots.

Nothing. At least he scared away the hawk.

All Chris's calves were named after the month they were born. It was easy to remember who was who.

His two big workhorses, one white, the other black, were good workers. One morning on a freezing winter day some of us went with Chris to Woodinville Train Station to pick up apple trees. The horses, hooked up to the buggy, had no problems. But it was freezing to everyone else.

"Pound your feet on the floor," Chris yelled. "Don't let them freeze."

I almost froze, but we finally made it back home. Everyone thawed out in a tub full of hot water. Well, one at a time we thawed out, maybe two at a time. At least there were no casualties.

The blacksmith shop held many wonders and mysteries. The fire pit was where Chris would heat up horseshoes red hot, hammer so hard, and shape them to near perfection.

To sharpen his tools, sickles, blades on the hay cutter, knives, axes anything dull. Chris had the answer. The grinding stone wheel was no ordinary wheel. With a right-foot, left-foot pedal, the grinding stone wheel could spin fast as Chris sharpened away. Round and round it would go. An old coffee can filled with water as nailed to the wall above with a small nail hole, slowly dripping water on the grinding stone wheel. One thing I didn't like—the seat was too hard.

Chris said, "You try pedaling."

My legs were too short. I could not reach the pedals. But I could stand on one side of the pedals and ride up and down.

Round the corner of the blacksmith shop there was a tall, narrow, unusual building. This was the outhouse. It was called an "outhouse" because it was "outside" of the house. This made sense to me. But what a surprise when I had to use the outhouse. Thousands of people must have used it and not one person flushed the toilet! Peeking down, I thought the smell, the flies, were awful!

Besides, there was no toilet paper, only a Sears Roebuck catalog. I only used the outhouse for emergencies.

Not only domestic animals roamed around the property; there were wild ones too. The older boys almost caught a "wild" pig with sharp, curved horns by its mouth. But the pig was too fast and escaped.

In the fall, the "fuzzy, wuzzy" caterpillars wiggled along. Reddish-brown with round black stripes, these little creatures felt soft, furry and friendly. Like the potato beetle, the caterpillar would roll up and play dead in your hand.

I liked to catch snakes. These were not rattlesnakes from eastern Washington with a bite that could kill. (I did hear about a rattler that crawled all the way over the Cascade Mountains into western Washington.) Bothell snakes were just garter snakes, harmless with bright-color stripes. Different colors, different family. They could slide fast! Often, I would lose them in the grass. After playing with a snake, woo oh! Your hands would stink! They stank for a long time.

Daddy Long Legs, now there's a "bug." I have always liked that name, a daddy with long legs. Then there's the centipede. Have you tried counting the legs of a centipede as it was moving? Impossible.

Tent caterpillars must like large families. There were hundreds, thousands living together in white, silky webs on trees, especially apple trees. They all looked the same, brown with yellow stripes. So many caterpillars! A clump in your hand felt weird. But they didn't bite little boys.

Lizards and salamanders looked alike, well, yes and no. The lizard had full, brownish-gray, dry skin, four feet with little toes, a long tongue, and was afraid of boys. As soon as I tried to capture one, zip! back into the rocks. I wanted to hold one so bad!

Salamanders were different. While I was digging in the rich, black dirt by Chris's barn, a gorgeous salamander flipped up suddenly without warning. Frightened, I didn't know what it was. But I knew it was a beauty: wet, dark-black skin, a bright yellow stripe from his head to tail, not at all like a lizard. The best part was he liked me. I could hold him in the palm of my hand and he was not afraid; he did not run. We were friends, friends for a while.

Something was strange one day. All of a sudden, I had foster brothers. I didn't know where they had come from. I resented the fact that they called MY mom and dad their "mom and dad." No, my mom was not their mom and my dad was not their dad

At an early age I had to sleep with a foster brother. He spit in my face and laughed. That was a terrible feeling, somebody's saliva rolling down your cheek. Thank goodness it only happened once in my lifetime.

In years ahead, I would accept my foster brothers as true brothers. Each boy had his own story of heartache, pain and sorrow. I was the lucky one.

Besides the horses and buggy, my neighbor Chris had two cars. The Ford Model A was bought from the showroom for three hundred dollars, it sputtered and purred like a sewing machine. The inside windows had little cloth curtains with a soft ball on a string to pull them down. The upholstery and interior smelled, smelled just like an old Model A.

His other car was actually a truck, about a 1927 Chevy truck. The sides had a canvas to roll up for easy side hauling.

The happy times of a boy running in the pasture, walking in the woods, discovering little creatures, carefree, would soon be partially interrupted by school.

Kindergarten, here I come!

# Chapter 4
# Starting School – Learning to Learn

It was either a "curse" or a "blessing in disguise"; my birthday missed the eligibility date to start school. My sister Pat started the next year with me. Little did I understand what this meant. We went to school together, brother and sister, in grade for twelve years.

If kindergarten was a prep school for first grade, I think maybe I flunked. All I learned was how to drink milk, eat graham crackers for a snack, and head on the desk for a nap. Oh yes, the big, huge black pencils were fun to use to write numbers and try to write the letter "A." Maybe kindergarten helped in some preparation.

The fact that I was eleven months older than my sister or, as she would point out, the same age for three weeks, caused a crisis in first grade. The teacher was taking a survey. She wanted to know how many twins were in the class. A photographer from the Bothell Citizen was coming to take pictures of twins in school. She insisted Pat and I were twins! I insisted we were not! I was eleven months older! As much as the teacher kept insisting, I kept resisting!

"OK. Let's go to the principal's office," the teacher growled as she grabbed my hand and pulled me to the office.

Of course, I was right. It was my first time to the principal's office. It wouldn't be the last.

Elementary school was a time friendships developed and would continue to grow until high school graduation. Two of my best friends I met in elementary school were Rich and Joe. Rich was the son of an insurance executive at Bothell State Bank. Joe was the son of the Superintendent of Bothell Schools. I was proud to be the son of a meat cutter.

When Rich was in the second grade, I was invited to his house for party. I was completely surprised!

Not only did he receive gifts but everyone else at the party received gifts too!

Mine was a bright-red plastic twin-engine airplane. And it wasn't small, it was big!

A picture in the Bothell Citizen brought me short fame as a fifth grader. An election was coming up, a "special two-mill levy to keep the library functioning." Our class just happened to be at the library several blocks from the school. Four of us were photographed with books in our hands and smiles on our faces.

I will never forget the book I was reading. It was quite a story about why black people have curly, fuzzy hair! It seemed long ago in Africa a tribe was out hunting in the desert. A fierce wildfire had everyone surrounded. The tribesmen dug into prairie dog holes, but the tops of their heads didn't fit. As the fire swept overhead, every one's hair was singed. From that day forward, blacks have had curly, the illustrations were very graphic. For me it made pretty good sense. What was there?

One of my favorite places to visit as a child was Uncle Fred and Aunt Clara's house. Uncle Fred was a lieutenant colonel in the U.S. Army. But he wasn't just army officer. He was a Korean War hero. As he was crossing a river with his men in Korea they were ambushed. Uncle Fred was shot in the leg. When he was told to retreat and fly out for a medical help, he refused to go. He had to stay and fight with his men. As, a result, his leg had to be amputated later.

The first time I saw the "wooden leg," it fascinated me to no end. Of course, I had to touch, knock, and eventually slide down his "leg." Uncle Fred used to laugh would almost always lose my balance and end up on the floor. Because of his smile and gentle manner, I was proud to be his nephew. Uncle Fred was a subconscious influence on another trip to the library. I found a book entitled *22 Stayed*. This was the first book to give me a lasting and profound fascination for people. It planted seeds for my own writing tastes and style.

The book *22 Stayed* documented twenty-two prisoners of war of the Korean Conflict; twenty-two soldiers who did not want to return to the United States but wanted to stay in North Korea. The author wrote about each in separate chapters. They were mini-biographies.

At the time I didn't know too much about brainwashing. But the thought that someone would choose to stay in the country of their captors was unbelievable.

Every time POWs of the Vietnam War were mentioned in the news, I thought about *22 Stayed*. What was going on at Hanoi Hilton?

Spelling was an early subject I didn't care too much for in elementary school. When the teacher asked us to take out our spelling books, anger swelled within me. I hated spelling! Probably because spelling required homework and two things no boy needed to be bothered with. After school, I needed to play in the woods.

I lifted up the desk, pulled out my book, put the desk top down, and slammed the book on the desk. I had not intended the noise to be so loud.

The teacher immediately looked up.

"What's the matter, Gene? Don't you like spelling?"

I quickly snapped back, "I didn't say a word!"

"You don't have to say a word," the teacher replied. "Actions speak louder than words."

Ever since I have been reminded numerous times how indeed our actions speak louder than our words. I found myself quoting that statement throughout my life, not only verbally but also in my mind.

One of the favorite songs I learned early in school was a kick to sing:

"Old Dan Tucker." It was a kick to sing:
Old Dan Tucker was a mighty man
He washed his face in a frying pan
He combed his hair with a wagon wheel
And he died with a toothache in his heel
So get out of the way Old Dan Tucker
You're too late to stay for supper
Supper's over, breakfast a cookin'
Old Dan Tucker standin' a lookin'

But the song to sing as a group in bed was a close second favorite:

Ball, ball, ball
The score was six to nothing

The beetles were ahead
The bed bugs made a homerun
And knocked me out of
Bed, bed, bed!

And the bed bugs knocked all of us out of the bed to the floor!

After school and weekends there was plenty of free time to play. The woods always captured our imagination. We would build "camps" out of ferns; fern roofs and fern walls. There were ferns all over!

Then we would divide into cowboys and Indians. Guns were not allowed in the home, not even toy guns. So we made guns out of branch twigs. And sometimes we'd find a piece of wood that looked like a rifle. It was hard at times to pick what was going to be "King of the Wild Frontier" or "the Lone Ranger."

One day, playing by myself, I headed toward the corner of the wood where I could look down and see the blacksmith shop. One tree next to the road and pasture always caught my attention. It was so, so tall, with outstretched arms reaching for the sky. I had always wanted to climb this tree, but had trouble building the nerve. This day I was going to climb! With its low-hanging branches, it was easy to start.

I developed an excellent rhythm. Right foot, step on branch, reach with hand to closest branch. Left foot, step on branch, reach with left hand to closest branch. Push legs, pull up arms. I did this over and over again, but slowly. Halfway up the tree, I noticed pitch covering my fingers. That was OK.

Near the top I paused. All this time, I had been looking upwards to the next branch to catch.

As I looked down, a panic attack briefly engulfed me. I was high, higher than I'd ever been! How was I going to climb down?

I reversed my rhythm. Gently lowering feet to branches I could not see, only feel, my descent was careful. The climb up was faster than the climb down. As the ground became closer, I started feeling more secure. Standing on the ground under the tree, glancing up, I was happy I had finally climbed the tree of my dreams. It was the first and last "tall" tree I would ever climb.

Summertime meant two sure things—hay and cherries.

Chris grew hay on several acres of our pasture. When it was time to cut, everyone helped. First, he would take his horse-drawn hay cutter, with a blade like a haircutter only longer and bigger, and cut the hay. With pitchforks, hay was stacked in mounds as high as possible.

Then Chris hitched the horses onto the huge wagon and all the hay mounds were thrown in. Part of the fun work belonged to the little kids in the wagon. Our responsibility was to jump on the hay to pack it down for more room.

The bonus came in the barn. From as high as we dared, anyplace in the barn, we jumped to pack the hay again.

Chris also had several acres of cherry trees. To my disappointment they were mostly sour pie cherry trees. But what about the Bing cherry tree! I could climb, sit and eat for hours the most scrumptious, sweet cherries in the world. Only problem, face and hands smeared with Bing juice was evidence of guilt—wonderful guilt.

When the cherries were ripe to pick, teenagers and even kids like me could learn some spending money. Usually after picking only a few flats, I would turn them over to Chris for payment. At twenty-five cents a flat, fifty cents is all I needed for a day's work. I'd jump on my bike; take the back gravel road to Bothell. If only those dogs wouldn't chase me!

First stop was Meredith's Five and Ten. They always had great items and were not too expensive. Later in life I learned that Washington State's Senator Patty Murry's father owned that store.

On the corner of Main Street sat Crawford's Drugstore. Can you believe this? On a penny sale, you could buy something and get the second one for a penny Isn't that a bargain? I bought a comb and the second one was a penny.

Not only was Crawford's famous for one-cent sales, their sit-down counter served genuine chocolate Cokes and cherry Cokes. Nothing imitation. Real chocolate, real cherry, and "hand stirred."

Next day I'd be back in the cherry orchard. The incentive to pick more cherries increased.

Another summertime ritual was blackberry picking. We started with an empty pail and in a short time it was full. Blackberry bushes were growing everywhere. One large bush was home to a pheasant family and a quail family—gorge us birds, especially the white ring around the pheasant.

Back at the house, all buckets were emptied so Mom could start baking mouthwatering blackberry pie and tangy blackberry jam. I couldn't get enough!

After a weekend of playing in the woods, on Monday I just had to tell teacher everything. I rambled on about the fern camps, how much fun it was pulling the ferns, building the camps, and playing cowboys and Indians.

When I had finished, the teacher said, "Show me your hands."

As I turned my hands over for closer inspection, she surprised me. "You must have been playing hard. I see scratches and calluses all over your hands."

In the fifth grade, I came to realize there were a masculine "Gene" and a feminine "Jean." Jean was a girl who had a desk right behind mine. If the teacher called on me with a question, and I didn't know the answer, I would turn around and look at the girl. But soon the teacher got tired of the game and started to call me by my last name.

"Mr. Olson."

It was also at this time my "love life" slowly started to evolve. At first, I was a messenger or "carrier for the other boys' love notes. It was fun at first, but soon became a nuisance. Having a sister so close to my age would prove to be a treasured asset. From the fifth grade all the way through high school, she was many times a precious link.

The first crush in elementary school was with one of the twins in my class Brooke. They were identical except one had a beauty mark close to her mouth. She was the one I liked. I found a "friendship" ring with red hearts all around it and wanted to give it to her. Being oh-so-shy, I didn't know how to approach her.

An older foster brother was quick to give me advice. "Roll the ring on the floor so it goes under her desk. Then pick it up and say, 'Look at this ring I found. Do you want it?'"

I practiced and practiced the advice. As recital time approached, the fifth grader fizzled. I couldn't do it. My "crush" would soon be over. And would never know.

It was about this time, in 1957, when I was eleven years old, that my parents decided to divide the property in half and build a new house. After selling the old house, we rented a house in Kenmore during construction of the new one.

Kenmore was a small, nearby community on the northeast end of Lake Washington. On a hill in Uplake Terrace, the rental didn't have woods or forests but there was a great view of Lake Washington. Plus, our house was under the direct flight path of seaplanes gliding into Kenmore Air Harbor. They skimmed clos over the house—real close!

A quarter of a mile down the hill from the house there was a large, vacant dirt lot ideal for baseball games. One afternoon a game of softball started. I usually didn't play catcher, but I was trying my best to catch. When a fast pitch came zooming right over the plate the better swung and missed. My glove missed the ball also. The fast ball hit square between my legs, hitting my balls; not baseballs, my balls!

Crying, I lay in the dirt with unbearable pain; no, it was tormenting pain; no, it was excruciating pain; actually no words could describe how I felt!

My memory was lost. Two older boys, one my brother, carried me up the hill to home. The next thing I recalled, I was in bed still with pain and a doctor was examining someplace between my legs. Oh the pain! My scrotum was swollen brighten red the size of a balloon. The pain did not cease overnight. Over days a slight, very light easing appeared.

From the bed I graduated outside to the fish pond. The fresh air, wicker chair and a few books kept me company. There were no fish in the pond, all had died. We even tried stocking it with bullheads caught from the Sammamish Slough. They also died and smelled rotten.

A few months later I would be helping print "1957" in the fresh cement at our new house in Bothell.

Sitting among the trees, especially the one I had bravely climbed, overlooking the pasture, our new two-story home also came with a new address, 20208 Bothell Way NE, Bothell, WA 98011.

Thank goodness the bulldozer left my favorite tree alone. Cars in the parking area could rest next to my evergreen tree.

The master bedroom and girls' bedrooms were upstairs. All the boys' room were downstairs with bunkbeds in the rec room. The living room upstairs even had brick fireplace. Everything was new! A contrast from the old house.

As a toddler, the trips to Gramma's house were exciting. We even had to drive over the Cascade Mountains through Snoqualmie Pass to Spokane, Washington. The mountains were high and scary. I kept wondering what would happen if the car went off the cliff!

Eastern Washington was not like Bothell. It was always hot in the summer.

Everything was dry and brown. The grasshoppers were as big as birds. And there were true rattlesnakes!

But Spokane had something Bothell didn't— SODA POP! We never had a soda pop at home, but Gramma Olson always had the refrigerator fully stocked.

During my junior high school days, Gramma Olson moved in next door to Chris's rental house. It was newer than her house in Spokane. And she was living o close.

Every day after school my sister and I would practice our musical instruments at Gramma's. My sister played the clarinet. I played a slide trombone. Well I tried to play. I'm sure I could have done better if private lessons were available. Then time was up, Gramma Olson gave us a snack. The snack was always the same, strawberry jam on saltine crackers and a small can of Tree Top Apple Juice.

Gramma Olson's first name was Carrie. Of course we never called her by her first name. She came from Sweden and our great-great-grandmother from Sweden had lived to be ninety-five years old—and she smoked a pipe!

I was intrigued by Gramma's old wooden radio. The dial had places like "Tokyo, Moscow, Amsterdam," etc. As hard as I tried, I could never hear anything from those exotic places.

One afternoon of music practice, I was surprised, genuinely surprised. Gramma Olson always had her hair braided and rolled up in a bun on the back of her head. This the only way we saw her hair. My sister and I were seated at the table having our snack. The door to the bathroom was half opened. I could not believe my eyes! Gramma was combing her pure white hair. Her hair was half an inch from the floor! What had happened to her bun? How had her hair gotten so long?

My aspirations to be a trombonist ended when I made a tape recording on the family's Weber reel-to-reel. It sounded awful! I have never picked up a trombone since.

All my closest buddies turned out for the Little League team. They mad the first team and I ended up on the farm team, just barely good enough to make the team.

Junior high school was the same way in sports. I was good enough to take the basketball team, but never the starting five. However, I always played the last two minutes of a game. I was a professional "bench warmer."

The seventh grade was a nice switch from being in the same classroom day after day. Different teachers, different students, different subjects.

Of course, I had to fall in love with one teacher. She was so beautiful…just so beautiful! I had never seen such big, wide lips before. She wore the brightest lipstick ever made. She was tiny and always dressed in a sweater or blouse with short skirts. I wouldn't say she had an "hourglass figure." She looked better than that.

The seeds for my interest in writing were sown in junior high school. Not only could you write on the journalism staff you could also help "publish" and distribute the school newspaper, The Bobcat.

The publishing consisted of blue stencils (typewriter-made impressions), a mimeograph machine (always broken down), a stapler with extra staples and two fast hands. Everything went quite smoothly until the mimeograph machine broke down. I decided writing for the paper was far better than publishing. From that day, even throughout college, I have been involved in journalism or creative writing.

The biggest drawback in junior high school was the concept of homework. I never thought much of the idea. My goal was to do the bare minimum, just enough homework to squeak by. Sometimes I could "bluff" my way through. But most often I had to face the consequences.

During class sessions, and this occurred early in elementary school, I found it very hard to concentrate. Spring was the roughest. How lucky I felt to be assigned a desk near the window! But before the year had ended, I was usually in the front row or at least away from the window. This did not stop my "daydreaming," it only switched the topic. And there were always plenty of topics.

Physical education in the ninth grade was my best subject, along with journalism. I was not a super athlete, but enjoyed the fun and competition.

One day, after everyone had showered and was getting dressed, Rich, my best friend, and I were "horsing around." We ended up back-to-back with Rich's arm around my neck. He lifted me up so my feet were off of the floor. Soon I could not breathe and fell limp to the concrete, hitting my head. I passed out.

Of course, everyone was staring at me when I gained consciousness. "Is Gene alive or dead?"

At the next class the teacher was concerned, "Gene, you have an awful cut above your eye. Let's put a Band-Aid on it."

Rich was quick to protest.

"Gene, you don't need a Band-Aid. God will heal it."

After listening for a while, I realized Rich made sense. God could heal it. This is when I first discovered my best friend Rich was a Christian Scientist. The scar above my eye would not be the last.

Some friends lived on Lake Sammamish. In elementary school I had taken swimming lessons at Juanita Beach on Lake Washington. It was shallow water for a long distance out. But I had only learned how to face float and back float. A Lake Sammamish I became skilled in dog paddling. It was great! I could stay on top of the water and move around, just like regular swimming!

I learned to swim the crawl stroke at a boys' dreamland. My parents found a little cabin on Lake Roediger. The lake was 254 acres north of Monroe in the foothills of the Cascade Mountains. Mount Pilchuck was visible above the tree line Lake Roediger was three lakes divided by small, shallow channels. Boats could float slowly between the lakes, but usually had to pull up the outboard motors so they couldn't scrape the bottom rocks.

At first, there was a log blockhead on the lakeshore. Then a backhoe came, knocked out the old wood and presto, a beach! There was a sandpit near with all the free sand we needed.

Early in the morning the lake was smooth as glass. A dip at 7:00 a.m. before breakfast was invigorating in the warm water. Even in the rain, the water temperature was pleasant. We would swim rain or shine.

The old rowboat had plenty of use fishing, dawn to dusk. Rainbow trout were planted by the state and there were also bass, perch and yes, bullhead. In the evening or early morning I liked to row quietly on the lake with a dry fly on a long line. It would make a "V" shape on the smooth surface of the water. You could see when the fish was making a strike at the fly. Sometimes I was successful, most otter times, not so successful.

The old rowboat also joined in our swimming. We would tip it over, dive underneath and come up under its air pocket. It was scary, but only at first.

What a difference in the old rowboat when we bought a used $7^{1}/2$ h horsepower Evinrude outboard motor. Goodbye oars! Now the old rowboat had speed. Full throttle put wind in our faces. We could sail to the other two lakes with ease.

The channel was shallow going into the second lake. And the second part was so much different, hundreds of water lilies extending from the shore to near middle. It was extremely shallow with a muddy bottom. An oar could be pushed down and still not find the bottom.

Going into the third lake we had to lift up the motor and paddle through. This lake was larger than the one our cabin was on, and it had a better view of Mount Pilchuck. I could tie the boat up on this part of the lake, walk a little way up a road, and buy some gasoline at the only lake store.

With spring came Momma duck and her babies. How cute the baby ducks were following their mom in an orderly single file! All you had to do was give out a loud "QUACK" and everyone would come paddling. We saved all old bread for these precious ducklings. Not one of them was ugly!

When we heard otters liked to swim underneath the water, grab baby ducks by their feet, pull them under and eat them, we became baby duck defenders. Whenever we saw an otter swim toward the ducks, from shore we'd throw rocks, in the boat we'd splash the oars. The otters always became frightened and quickly submerged.

About four docks to the left of our cabin there was a couple oblivious anyone or anything on the lake. They were always on the dock kissing; first she was lying on top of him, the next minute he was on top of her. We figured it could only be one thing—they were on a honeymoon! We tried not watching, but that was futile.

From a rowboat with oars, to a 7 ½ horsepower outboard, the next in line was a thirty-five Evinrude outboard-powered Owen's ski boat. The 7 ½ outboard was fast on the rowboat. The thirty-five Evinrude outboard zoomed fast on the fifteen-foot ski boat.

And that is what we did, ski. There was a mandatory speed limit on the Ike to protect fishermen; eight miles per hour until 10:30 a.m. and then eight miles per hour after 5:30 p.m. It was tragic waiting for 10:30 to roll around. It was even tragic to have to stop skiing at 5:30.

At twelve years old, I learned how to water ski on two skis. The trick was to lean back, bend the knees, keep the arms straight and the rope between the skis; when slack was out of the rope yell "hit it" or make a "thumbs up" sign. The driver throttled full speed, you let the rope pull you out of the water and gradually stood up, but you had to keep the skis ahead of you or else you would fly forward.

The next step was one ski. Once you could waterski on two skis, it was time for one. Your right foot would have the main one ski. While cruising on

36

two skis'; you just flipped off the left ski. You slowly placed your left foot in the rear molding of the right ski. That was it; very easy.

Finally, you learned on just one ski how to ramp off the dock standing in a starting position. You had to remember to closely watch the slack in the tow rope. When you were ready, you yelled "hit it" or gave thumbs up, and just as the slack tight, jumped in the water. This might take several attempts until coordination smoothed out.

I had many falls, many eyelashes pressed inside my eye, but many more of sheer joy!

# Chapter 5
# Bothell Senior High School –
# Fun and Friends

The three years at Bothell Senior high School could not be characterized as "academic enlightenment." My study habits were poor, usually just cramming before exams. I was an excellent "crammer." A grade point average was nothing to take seriously. The academic world was foreign. A thirst for knowledge only existed on the horizon.

However, I did excel in other areas: student government, journalism, friends, fun, friends, and more fun.

The first week of high school an assembly was held in the cafeteria for all sophomores. The main purpose was to nominate class officers. A friend of my sister's nominated me as a candidate for class president. It was later revealed she had a "crush" on me.

There was not much campaigning; in fact I don't recall any posters, just a speech before the students. I guess I did OK, or had more friends than I thought, because I won the election.

The first official public duty as class president proved a disaster. There was going to be a general assembly in the gymnasium for the entire student body. I had to make an announcement concerning homecoming activities for the Sophomore Class. The assemblies were usually held at the end of the day. Stress kept building as I thought about what I was going to say.

A bell rang and the announcement for an assembly hit my nerves. First time before a large audience; I had notes prepared on several three-by-five cards.

Almost reaching the gymnasium, I stopped fast. I had to use the restroom! I had to use the restroom badly! Walking fast, I made it just time. I placed my three-by five cards on top of the urinal; this was a big mistake! They fell down a small crack in back of the urinal. The crack was so thin! Lost! My stress level jumped higher!

Walking into the gymnasium, what did I see? There was no podium to hide behind. Standing way out close to the center of the basketball court was a lovely, Elvis Presley-type microphone on a slim post. And that was it!

Now the big "if only" came. If only I had those three-by-five cards!

"Now, the sophomore class president, Gene Olson, has an announcement to make."

I wished I had a podium, but there wasn't much I could do now. As I started to speak, a nervous twitch developed in my right leg. It started shaking. My first reaction was, "Everyone can see it; I'd better say something.

"I don't know why my leg is shaking, it just is." Everyone laughed and I continued on.

It was a tough incident to forget. Some students called me "Crazy Legs Olson" and others said I shouldn't have said anything since they couldn't tell my legs were shaking. Soon it was all forgotten.

Like many talents, public speaking is refined by repetition. At the end of the year I had confidence speaking and thinking on my feet. And those legs were still! Plus, I never had to use three-by-five cards.

Teenagers—first driver's license and first car. I was one of those!

My parents always said I could have a car, with one exception. They would never pay for it; the money was my responsibility. However, they would pay car insurance.

A member of the church worked part-time from his garage on slightly wrecked cars and resold them. He was going to be on the lookout for a nice "wreck" for me. The anticipation was almost too much for a teenager to bear

When news came, I was in "heaven." The treasure he found was a red and white hardtop convertible '55 Chevy. It was only "wrecked" on the right section headlight.

The red and white interior upholstery was immaculate. The radio had one of the first scanners, a Wonder Bar you pressed to find stations.

I always dropped by to see the progress. My heart ached! Soon completion time came. The fresh red and white paint made the '55 look showroom condition. But I couldn't drive it! I had no driver's license! The problem would soon be solved I turned sixteen.

I drove the driving test in my "new" '55 Chevy. Having enrolled in driver's training at school, it was easy.

From age fifteen with a special work permit, I worked in nearby Mountlake Terrace at Foodland Grocery "bagging" groceries, stocking shelves, sweeping and mopping floors.

Of course, the grocery business was different in the sixties. There were no scanners or self-service check-out. A customer could request paper bags or card board boxes. There were no plastic bags. The bagboy always carried the groceries to t sometimes getting a tip, usually about twenty-five cents.

Bagging groceries was an art. Heavy items, cans, etc., on the bottom, followed by lighter items, cereal boxes, etc., and bread, eggs, tomatoes on the very top. I used to get tired of hearing, "Now don't squish the bread!"

"Careful with the eggs!"

"Don't squeeze the tomatoes" and on and on. But as a professional, it didn't bother me. Besides, I was one of the fastest baggers in the store.

So this is how I was able to buy a car. I saved and saved and saved. I'm sure my friend at church could have sold the '55 Chevy for more than the six hundred dollars for which he sold it to me.

I drove my car, my first car, with pride. Washing and waxing was not work. I'd park the car in the back row at the Foodland parking lot so I could see it as I carried out groceries. You could say I was a "teenager in love!"

Driving the family car, a '53 Cadillac, down Pontius Road, I was distracted by a yellow jacket. Not wanting to get stung, I tried killing it on the dashboard. All my attention was on the bee and not on the road. I ended up on a deep ditch. Being half on the road and half in the ditch, the car could not move. A tow truck had to be called.

My mother was not very sympathetic.

"I don't understand why you would go into the ditch because of a bee."

"Mom, have you ever been stung by a bee?"

She answered "No."

Without thinking I said, "I wish someday you would get stung."

Working in the yard the next day, Mom stepped on a yellow jackets' nest and was stung fifty times on the leg!

The intensity of a "first love" or major infatuation changes a teenager's casual life into turmoil. It happened to me.

She lived in Kenmore, Uplake Terrace, a few houses up from where we had rented. Her home was large with a great view of Lake Washington.

I couldn't fully understand the attraction or infatuation, but she had something. She had something besides a pretty face. It was something I wanted to be with.

The first (the first time is always the hardest) I met her parents I was in or a surprise. After talking to her father, I found out he was in the pinball business. All the pinball machines in Seattle and surrounding area bars and taverns had his name on the front glass. But that wasn't the surprise.

Just as I was leaving, her father asked to speak privately.

"I was young once. If you have sex with my daughter, I hope you'll use some type of protection."

Sex with his daughter! That was the last thing on my mind. In fact, it wasn't even the last thing, it was a non-thing. Actually, for the sixties, her father was way ahead of his time.

After a date one night we stayed later in the car to "talk." Soon the talk turned into passionate kissing and hugging. With the windows all steamed over, we could see her mother flicking the porchlight as a signal for her daughter to come in.

And we couldn't see who was tapping on the window!

But we did hear, "It's time to come in!"

It didn't take long to receive my first moving violation. It was with the "pinball girl." I pleaded my case with the Seattle policeman.

"But Officer, the light was yellow when I went through."

"Young man, the light turned red on the trunk of your car. Here's the ticket."

Red on the trunk of my car? I took the ticket.

In the evening, my girlfriend's father wanted to help me out of the citation.

"I have some friends on the Seattle Police Department. Maybe I can pull a few strings."

He called the police headquarters and asked for a certain officer. My ears perked up.

"Can you help out my daughter's boyfriend on a ticket? I have a bottle of whiskey for you."

Back in the room he said, "There's nothing we can do. The officer turned in his ticket book, otherwise…"

At this time, I wasn't fully aware of my girl's father's involvement in pinball machines and who knows what. There was a big shake-up with corruption and vice the Seattle Police Department. Payoffs, bribes, corruption, illegal gambling, anything to make money.

Anyone under eighteen in Seattle receiving a ticket could go to the courthouse for a safety lecture. The ticket was then erased from the records.

This was appealing. I hadn't driven too often in downtown Seattle, but this was important. When I arrived at the courthouse around 3:45 p.m., most of the parking places along the street were full. Then I got lucky spotting one lonely spot.

The lecture had nothing to say I didn't already know. I was happy to leave boring courthouse after an hour.

Running across the street to where I had parked my car, panic set in. It wasn't there! Someone had stolen my Chevy!

Approaching the parking meter, my eyes focused on a little sign with small red lettering, "NO PARKING 4:00 TO 6:00 p.m. Violators' cars will be towed away." This did not appeal to me! My '55 Chevy had been impounded!

Time came when I wanted my parents to meet my girl's parents over dinner. It sounded like a good idea.

Dad's response, "NO!"

I should never have told him about "fixing" the ticket and the whiskey bottle!

My response, "And you call yourself a Christian! You won't even meet my girlfriend's parents!"

It was in the afternoon. I raced out of the house, jumped in my Chevy, and took off toward town. I was boiling! Dad's temperature was also rising.

Just before downtown Bothell there was a very sharp curve. As I swung around, I noticed my girlfriend's father coming the opposite direction. I waved and put on the brakes. He noticed and pulled off the road. I made a U-turn and parked behind him. Standing on the side of the road, talking, here came Dad barreling around the sharp curve. He stopped. Introductions were given. Dinner reservations were not.

Well, at least they had met.

Student conduct in the halls at Bothell High was getting "out of control" too much kissing, too much holding, too much physical contact. A new student regulation was issued by the administration: "No physical contact with the opposite sex allowed in the hallways."

Like any high school, in the morning Bothell High students gathered around lockers, talking, getting books, running here and there. I was trying to talk my girl. Because of the noise and confusion, I grabbed her arm and pulled her off to the side of the hallway.

Immediately, a little twerp teacher I did not recognize came up to me.

"Don't touch her. There's no body contact in the hallways."

That did it! I tried to explain I was just trying to get her out of the way. We rambled back and forth.

"Do you want to go to the office?"

"Sure, let's go."

The arguing continued, picking up heated momentum all the way to the office. The office staff looked up like "What is going on here?" The vice principal calmed us down and asked me to sit in his office. Ten minutes he returned.

"Everything OK, Gene?"

"Everything's OK."

"Go to class."

It wasn't exactly like the first grade when I had gone crying to the office accused of being a twin. But I did feel like I was back in the first grade!

After school I was taking my girl home to the Uplake Terrace hill. Joe, the school superintendent's son, came along for the ride.

I walked my girlfriend to the door, quickly returning to the car. The '55 Chevy was slowly moving down the hill! I grabbed for the door. It was locked. Joe was laughing! The only thing I could do was jump on the trunk. I had nothing to hang on to! The speed increased. At the bottom of the hill was a sharp curve. Since the car was in neutral, it was hard to drive. When the car swerved around the corner, I slid off the trunk, hit the pavement, and stretched out my arms to brace against sliding into the curb. Joe was still laughing!

Standing in line at the Burgermaster, the one and only burger place in Bothell known for excellent crinkle cut fries, I felt a small sting on my right hip. Pulling the sticky shirt away, I noticed a cut, a deep cut. But what was the white stuff? It was my hip bone!

I thought about my close friend, Rich, the Christian Scientist.

He would have said, "You don't need a Band-Aid, Gene. God will heal it."

I didn't put a Band-Aid on it. God healed it. But I sure could have used one! Another scar to remind me of Rich.

As teenage relationships go, it wasn't long before someone else caught my eye. It was at the Halls Lake Church of the Nazarene campground. Church services were held under a tent, sawdust and all.

Several teenagers had gathered in a small snack bar building. There she was, standing by herself. I didn't recognize this little beauty. What was going on here? Had I slipped up? Where had SHE come from? Oh, those big beautiful brown eyes dark hair, cute smile; I was smitten on the spot. Here we go again!

Her name was Vicki, daughter of an Air Force man. She lived in Mountlake Terrace, a short distance from Bothell. Since she went to Mountlake Terrace High School, she was a "Terrace Girl." And lucky for me, her home was only a few blocks from where I worked at Foodland Grocery.

Sometimes she would walk up to Foodland to buy cat food, and to see me and talk. Her dad used to tease her about going too far, when a store was just around the corner. I can visualize it now, I am dust mopping the floor, around the corner she struts, smiling and happy I'm there.

"Can you tell me where the cat food aisle is?"

The next thing I knew, she was sitting next to me in the '55 Chevy. And very night after work, I was stopping by her house.

After a date one evening, we both stood by the car. The time was perfect for the first goodnight kiss. For a moment we looked at each other. Then Vicki closed her eyes. I kept looking into her face, thinking, "I guess she wants me to kiss her." I kissed her. A single strand of her long hair got caught between our lips. It didn't matter. We liked each other.

On Halloween, Vicki's younger brother was sick. We decided to go trick-or-treating and give all the "treats" to him.

At the door we would bend down like smaller kids.

"Aren't you guys kind of old to be trick-or-treating?"

And to Vicki, "Don't I know you from my English class?"

The laughter never stopped!

Vicki's brother was surprised when we dumped all the trick-or-treat candy at the edge of the bed.

In my junior year, student body elections drew near. A friend and I decided to do something never attempted before in student body elections. We would run for president and vice-president on the same ticket, as Bullard and Olson.

Poster parties were organized. Our last name initials would be the theme —"VOTE FOR THE BO BOYS." Pictures of skunks were plastered throughout the school.

Unfortunately, we lost the election. But I believe we won for having the most original and creative campaign.

Another little beauty came crashing into my life. Nancy, daughter of my dentist, would be my last high school sweetheart. Her gracious style, cover-girl looks talent, especially her voice and piano playing, attracted me like no other. The attraction would only grow stronger.

However, I was at a dilemma. It would not be fair to have two girlfriends.

The time to break up with Vicki was hard and the most difficult decision I ever had to make with a girl. As she sat on the sofa with her long, black hair, brown eyes, eyelashes fluttering and black sweater accentuating her figure, I almost decided to change my mind. *Maybe I shouldn't break up after all,* I thought. *Maybe this was the wrong decision? Maybe I was really stupid?*

Then I thought about Nancy.

Sadly, I told Vicki, "There's another girl."

The daughter of my dentist had stolen my heart. I would pick her up in the morning for a ride to school and a ride home. Sometimes I would take her to music lessons in Kirkland.

One favorite place to go "talk" (and kiss) was the old road deep in cherry orchard. The place where I had picked cherries as a child was quiet and no one bothered us.

I stopped by Nancy's house one evening unannounced. We were alone for a while in the downstairs rec room, until her father entered.

"Gene, I think it's time for you to go home."

Was it because he had seen me kissing his teenage daughter?

Was it because he had seen his teenage daughter sitting on my lap?

Was it because his teenage daughter was in a robe?

I figured a combination of the three. I know it wasn't to go home and brush my teeth.

One Easter morning, Nancy sang "The Lord's Prayer" at my church in Seattle. It was beautiful. Her voice was a gift, a gift only God could give. I was proud,

Teenage years were rough, touch, confusing and full of surprises. And if you had an older sister by a couple of years, the rough, tough, confusion and surprises were exasperating.

"If only" my older sister, Aarlie, could have been just a little "normal," my teenage life would have been easier. No, she had to be the first female student body president, song leader, homecoming queen and Christmas tree queen—but things I could have dealt with.

Instead, she had to be on the speech and debate teams! Regional tournaments were not enough for her. She had to go to state tournaments and bring back fancy first-place trophies! The first-place trophy for extemporaneous speaking; anyone can speak extemporaneously! I got tired of seeing her lugging all these trophies home from school.

I'm not sure if comments from other people, "You guys look the most alike from anyone in the family," started the irritation. But something was festering. My sister took it upon herself to be Mom's advisor to me. She was not even appointed!

Sometimes I wanted to stay out late on the weekend or go someplace. My sister, the advisor, always had comments for Mom.

"Mom, I don't think that's a good idea."

"Mom, you should be more tough"

"Mom, Mom, Mom!"

I would become furious! Once I snapped back, "However I turn out, it's going to be your fault!"

Some say "Never debate a debater." But as a preteen, I used to wonder, peering out my window, why the old '54 green Ford was parked at night so long in the driveway! What was going on with my older sister and that ole pre-med student from University of Washington? Did Mom ever flip the porchlight to make her come in? No. Did Mom ever go down to the car, knock disruptively on the window, and tell my sister it was time to come in? No. And most importantly, did I ever advise on my sister's behavior? No.

Years later I would tease my brother-in-law, the orthopedic surgeon father of five, just what had he been doing in the car so late?

"Gene, we were studying the Bible."

He couldn't say it with a straight face. Maybe they were studying the Bible and got as far as, "In the beginning God created..."

Funny thing, I never saw the car windows steamed up!

As Senior Class President I was active in student government and also involved in the school newspaper, The Bothell Cougar.

The desire to write about sports, besides the enjoyment, was due to the lack of inspiration in my athletic career as a "barely made the team." I was better at writing than playing.

As sports editor, I also had a column named "Out of Gene's Pockets," with a bottom footnote "Off the Cuff." On the top of the column was a cartoon character with his pants pockets hanging out.

Writing sports, especially the column, brought great gratification. The only thing I didn't like and despised were the deadlines, too much pressure.

An advantage of being on paper staff was a permanent hall pass. I could go anyplace, anywhere, without faculty interruptions.

The journalism teacher was also the honors English teacher. Being his teacher's assistant gave me more time to work on the paper. As the class studied Tolstoy's War and Peace, I corrected test papers and left to do some writing.

Bothell High School made it to an important basketball playoff game. A radio sportscaster asked for help with player statistics, etc. He came to the school a day before the game, went over material, and asked me to sit next to him in the announcer's booth.

The game was close, exciting, filled with tension. The score went back and forth. At halftime the sportscaster asked for my comments on the radio. Well, of course I had a few words.

After finishing I saw, to my surprise, the entire Bothell section in the bleachers had turned round and was staring at me!

From radio I graduated to television, sort of. Bothell High had a Mock Political Convention in the gymnasium. I was a delegate from the state of Texas an gave the nominating speech for Lyndon Baines Johnson for President.

I tried to look "Texas," with a big cowboy hat, scarf, etc. Halfway through the speech, a Seattle news camera started filming close to the platform. Since I was speaking on civil rights, now was a good time to point my finger at the delegates below for a strong emphasis.

The evening news came on; there I was…well, does four seconds count? It was better than no seconds!

Bothell High had an exchange teacher from India, highly intelligent, with only a slight accent. In our current affairs class he was discussing different nationalities around the world. Of particular interest to me were his comments on the Scandinavian countries.

And the Norwegians were always fighting with the Swedes."

After his discussion, he asked each student to stand and say what nationality they were. This would prove America truly was a "melting pot."

When it was my turn, I stood up.

"I am half Norwegian and half Swede. And I get along with myself real well." That was good for a laugh from the other students!

There were more serious moments. The speech teacher stopped me in the hall.

"Gene, would you mind giving your persuasive speech to a sophomore class? I know it's quite religious, but I talked to the principal and he said it was OU."

I said, "Sure."

The title, "Why You Should Become a Christian."

The end of May, 1964, my last photograph would appear on the front page of The Bothell Cougar.

Gene Olson, Sue Johnson Capture 1964 ASB Award

Gene Olson and Sue Johnson are the 1964 recipients of the coveted ASB award, bestowed each year on two seniors for outstanding service to the school… He also had some comments on teenagers and standards. "I have always wondered why teenagers have to conform with everyone else. They are afraid to stand for their own beliefs if they are contrary to the 'crowd'… In my three years at Bothell High I have witnessed a problem that most teenagers are faced with. This problem is life. What is life? Some think it is a bottle of beer or engaging in activities at the drive-in. I'm glad that I discovered what life really is. To me life is Christianity. And Christianity in two words is Jesus Christ.

Graduation came. Everyone went their separate ways. Some would meet again. Some would die. No one would forget the Bothell Senior High School class of '64.

# Chapter 6
# Church and God

I consider myself half Norwegian, half Swede, half Democrat, half Republican, half catholic, half Protestant, and half a photographic memory.

The Roman Catholic Church says, "Raise a child up to twelve as a Catholic and he'll always be a Catholic."

I believe the same could be said in the Church of the Nazarene. "Raise a child up to twelve as a Nazarene and he'll always be a Nazarene."

The Church of the Nazarene was founded by Phineas Bresee in 1908 at Pilot Point, Texas. The church's doctrine is rooted in Wesleyan-Armenian theology. Their distinction from other mainline protestant churches lies in the belief of "entire sanctification." This is also called "Christian perfection," "perfect love," "heart purity," "the baptism with the Holy Spirit," "the fullness of the blessing," and "Christian holiness."

When you confess your sins to God and ask Him to come into your heart, a re-birth occurs, and you become a born Christian. Your physical body is not "born again," but a rebirth occurs in your mind and thinking toward God. It's almost like "starting from scratch."

Nazarenes believe "entire sanctification" or "perfect love" is "second work" from God. The Holy Spirit at this time cleanses the entire body and mind. Only God is perfect. As a Nazarene you "strive" daily for perfection as only Jesus the Nazarene was perfect.

It's true I won a prize for being the youngest baby at The Seattle first Church of the Nazarene. I have no remembrance.

I do remember numerous times sitting on a church pew—paper on a songbook, pencil in hand and drawing lines. As fatigue settled in, I would swing my legs up on the pew, place my head on Mom's lap and sleep. She always had a pencil plenty of paper and a soft lap.

The family transferred to Kirkland Church of the Nazarene. As a very small child I remember clearly standing with other children in front of the congregation. Each of us had lit candle with poster paper circled around the bottom to catch any dripping wax. We sang:

This little light of mine,
I'm gonna let it shine.
This little light of mine,
I'm gonna let it shine.
Let it shine, let it shine,
Let is shine.
Don't let Satan blow it out,
I'm gonna let it shine...

My main concern was the candle was dripping down. Would the poster paper stop the wax, or would the hot candle wax drip underneath and burn my hand? The paper worked.

To a child, church and God could be confusing. The idea of a "Holy Ghost" flying around was sometimes frightening. You could see "Casper the friendly ghost." He was friendly! But had anyone seen "the Holy Ghost" disappeared and "the Holy Spirit" took its place!

And as children we had to be careful talking about those "Pentecostal" people. Mom was raised in a Pentecostal church. Now what about those "holy Rollers? I thought maybe it was church where you could bring your roller skates and skate up and down the aisle during the preaching.

Then there was something called "speaking in tongues." I thought everyone spoke with a tongue. But this language...no one knew where it came from, except some guy in the back row.

Oral Roberts was the most famous "Pentecostalist" in the fifties. At eleven years old I'd watch him on a black-and-white portable TV just before bed. It was amazing! People were getting out of wheelchairs, healed! People were throwing away crutches, healed! All the sick running around, healed!

All Oral Roberts did was pray and lay his hands on these people. Something was happening.

But in my lifetime, I don't think I'd want to build a Gene Olson University.

Now we have seen televangelists Jim Baker fall, Jimmy Swaggart fall, and Bennie Hinn fall. No wait a minute. Bennie Hinn didn't fall, just false accusations? But the people Hinn blew of fell.

From Roberts laying on hands to Hinn blowing in the face, the crowds were and are the same. Only it went from black and white to color. The cameras and cameramen are more sophisticated. Oral Roberts was not so much concerned about attire.

Bennie Hinn always appeared in a slick, well-pressed, immaculate white suit.

I don't want to say anything negative against a "man of the cloth," or, should I say, a "man of white." Bennie Hinn reminds me of a minister I heard on the radio when I was about eleven years old. At the end of the program he gave this announcement:

"While praying yesterday god blessed me and he blessed my shirt. If you send in $9.95, I'll send you a piece of my blessed shirt."

Even as an eleven-year-old, I knew this was quite a statement. How many shirts was he wearing?

In 2005 I received an unsolicited letter from Tulsa, Oklahoma. It was addressed, "Dear…Someone connected with this Address." It was from a "church" and had an enclosed "prayer rug." Actually, it was picture of a prayer rug on paper. Basically, it said you had the rug for twenty-four hours and then returned it for another family "in need of a blessing" to use. And "be sure to have both knees on the rug when you pray."

Oh yes, the back page had places to check:
Pray for my family and me for

- My soul
- A closer walk with Jesus
- My health

Those were legitimate requests. But the list continued:

- A new car
- A money blessing
- Pray for God to bless me with this amount of money: $_____.

Of course, the last box to check in conclusion:

- Enclosed is my seed gift to God's work of $_____.

Seed gifts are exempt from the IRS. I just wonder what is going to sprout in Tulsa. I hope at least some seeds will survive.

Not much has changed from radio, television and mass mailings. Ministers, televangelists, schemers…some, not all, worship money and wealth as their God. It's easy. It's sad.

Around twelve years old, I became a born-again Christian. My body was not reborn, but my mind had rebirth. After confessing my sins and asking God to come into my heart, I felt a true presence of the Holy Spirit. This was the birth, the inception of a personal God, a personal relationship.

The concept or doctrine of entire sanctification is similar to becoming "Born-again."

Instead of "confessing sings," you ask God to "cleanse you" and He performs entire sanctification. But it does not stop there. It is a daily "walk" with God as you strive for perfection.

If you have problems with sin as a born-again Christian you are a "back-slider." If you have problems with sin as entirely sanctified, maybe you are a "back-back slider." I don't' know. I've never heard of that word.

In my childhood, boyhood and youth, church played a significant role in our family. We attended services on Sunday morning and Sunday night, and Wednesday night prayer meetings. No one was "forced" to attend church. It was choice, but if you decided once you did not want to attend church, lookout! Your choices were soon diminished to zero.

Traveling to Seattle first Church of the Nazarene brought our car along the new construction of the 1–5 Freeway running from California south to Canada north. The freeway was going to solve all the traffic congestion around Seattle. When the freeway opened, there was no congestion. Try driving north or south now on 1–5 morning or afternoon and it is a true parking lot.

I also had the chance of seeing the building of Century 21 World's Fair. It was going to be the biggest and greatest fair ever. But I had my doubts about the Space Needle's ability to remain standing. After its completion, Nancy and I had dinner in the restaurant, revolving every hour, with unbelievable views of Seattle. Once I was driving with my dad when I was twelve years old, on

Bothell Way Ne near the shores of Lake Washington and approaching Lake Forest Park.

He asked for the first time, "What do you want to be when you grow up?" "I don't know. I just want to work with people."

As a teenager, one night going to bed, I brought a Look magazine to read. The cover read, "Wanted: Priests, Rabbis and Ministers." I started reading about the future shortage of qualified men to lead in the Catholic churches, the Jewish synagogues and Protestant Churches.

For several days I couldn't stop thinking about the article. The "wanted" sign kept reappearing in my mind. I never mentioned the article to anyone.

Then I decided to talk with my minister.

"I'm glad you didn't say you had a dream or a vision. Not that God couldn't call in this way…"

Leaving the minister's office, I felt maybe God was calling me to be a minister.

There was a "wanted" sign.

# Chapter 7
# A Change in Course

After high school graduation I had no problems, no worries; life was carefree. Sitting on top of the mountain, the only thing I saw were clear blue skies. I was proud to have been a sophomore class president, senior class president, sports editor of the school newspaper and ASB award recipient, and that I had developed many close friendships from first grade to high school. The mountaintop did look good.

Northwest Nazarene College in Nampa, Idaho gave me a small activity scholarship. The amount made little difference in the yearly tuition. This summer was my last opportunity to earn money for college expenses.

Foodland was the only place to work. I liked "bagging" groceries better cleaning or sweeping floors. But cleaning and weeping were part of the job description.

On one sweeping assignment I came across a pack of cigarettes. It was similar to an incident that had occurred when I was eleven years old. Riding my bicycle to Bothell, I had seen something shiny on the shoulder of the road. I stopped, turned back and found a quarter. Next to the quarter was a pack of cigarettes. I picked up both and later at home smoked under the raspberry patch out of sight. My first cigarette.

Now, as I was sweeping the floor, I picked up the pack of cigarettes and put them in my apron. Only now I was seventeen, not eleven.

Afterwards I went to the back room and climbed some stairs to a small room with a one-way mirror to observe shoplifters. The thought came, "go ahead and try one." I was alone. I lit up. I felt sick. I was hooked!

A few days later I was invited to a party. Everyone was drinking alcohol, mostly beer. I drank my first beer.

For me, smoking and drinking were an eleventh commandment of "Thou shalt not...!" It was very close to "Thou shalt not kill." Maybe because the church looked so much at outward appearance and not what was inside the heart.

It was beyond comprehension. I could not conceive or envision stooping so low.

The scripture said, "Pride goeth before destruction." I was proud! My whole life seemed demolished. And where had God gone?

The summer flew fast; faster than I wanted. Just like in the first grade, my eleven month-younger sister was also preparing to enter Northwest Nazarene College.

The drive from Seattle to Nampa, Idaho, over the Washington Cascade Mountains, through Pendleton, Oregon, and the Blue Mountains took about eight hours. I was sitting in the back seat with Cathy on one side and my sister on the other. I'm not sure how it started, but Cathy and I were hidden under a pillow and she taught me how to French kiss. What a marvelous teacher! An eight-hour lesson I'll never forget

Nampa, Idaho, was a small town in the Treasure Valley near Boise. It was a lot like eastern Washington, no evergreen trees, a hot climate, farmlands and irrigational canals. The college was like a small oasis in the desert.

Besides the college, Nampa was "famous" for the Snake River Stampede Rodeo.

College life was foreign to me. I was no longer a BMC (Big Man on Campus); no one knew me and I didn't know anybody. Not only did I feel lost but also bewildered.

I was enrolled as a ministerial student; the conservative college forbade smoking or drinking alcoholic beverages as set forth in the manual of the Church of the Nazarene. But that didn't stop me from taking short walks down roads from the campus for a smoke.

My heart was not in "campus life." There was no thirst for knowledge or study habits to find knowledge. I felt out of place and the disinterest grew stronger each day. Missing classes, not reading textbooks, not turning in papers/assignments; I was a waste. And why did Psych 101 have to start before it was even light out?

When the Boise River was reaching flooding stage, calls went out for volunteer sandbaggers. This was a project where I could feel some accomplishment. The night was well spent. Why study and read books when a crisis was arising elsewhere? Plus, you could smoke and drink on the banks of the Boise River.

The "fun and friends" of high school were finally catching up with me. But not only was I drifting away from college academics I was also turning away from anything religious. And I was a ministerial student!

Several months passed with me wondering, "What on Earth am I doing in this Idaho town?" Some people are "saved by the bell"; I was "saved by the letter."

My sister received a letter from home "hinting" of financial concerns: maybe only one of us could continue at the college.

This was the only validation I needed to drop out of college and quit fooling myself and everyone else. Now was my chance. Perfect!

Naturally I had to be the martyr and tell my sister she should be the one to stay in college. Then she said I should be the one to stay.

After I convinced my sister, she was doing great as a college student, while I was doing poorly and was uninterested, she agreed to stay. I would make the sacrifice and leave.

A friend in college had a brother with an insurance company and a pesticide company in Boise. He worked part-time and more in the summer for his brother's pesticide company. He knew I could work with him part-time.

Boise, here I come!

I was not a rich man entering the big city. My recollection of money in my wallet was nonexistent. Unfortunately, my choice of housing was narrowed by a lack of monetary funds, or being broke. My apartment would not be a penthouse.

The only place I could find was directly across from the Idaho state capitol building. Just seven dollars a week, one dollar a day, perfect for my slim finances. To say it was an apartment was putting it mildly. It was more like a retirement center. The building was very old and so were its tenants. The bathroom was down the hall where the rustic communal refrigerator buzzed sometimes cold, sometimes warm.

With no air-conditioning, the second floor became worse than unbearable, but you still had to bear it.

Since there was no kitchen or stove, I ate my meals in a little café and never had enough to eat.

The pesticide work with my friend was OK, but went slow. While he was doing the spraying, I went to the neighbors.

"We're doing some pesticide spraying in the area and thought maybe you'd like your yard and trees sprayed too?"

Little did people realize, spray one yard and all the insects just crawled over into the neighbor's yard.

My salary was meager. What money I had went to beer and some more beer. Usually in a drunken stupor, I would turn to my Bible and the Book of Psalms.

*How long wilt thou forget me O LORD? forever? how long wilt thou hid thy face from me?*

(Psalm 13:1)

*My God, my God, why has thou forsaken me? Why art thou so far from helping me…?*

(Psalm 22:1)

This place in my Bible still shows the effects of beer tears—pages of beer tears. Are they worth anything?

In the evenings, with no money or anything to do, I would wander across the street to the state capitol park. Benches were scattered throughout the area. I'd sit down, observe people passing by. Two old men sharing peanuts with the pigeons

One day, I had to face reality and I didn't like what I saw. It wasn't a "mere existence." I had no life, no goals, no opportunities…I was just stagnant. I wanted out, again.

I retreated to the Bible one night, searching; I wasn't too sure what book I wanted to read. The story of the prodigal son looked like a good one. It reminded me of myself. I had been squandering my life at college and now these past few months, wasted. I started to read.

*And he came to himself*

Had I come to myself?

Yes, I had. I had turned away from God – mainly because of a proud heart. Yes, I had come to myself.

*I will arise and go to my father.*

Yes, that was what I would do. Not only go to my heavenly Father but also to my earthly father.

*I have sinned against heaven and before thee*

I was a sinner.

My mind was made up. In the morning I would leave. The prodigal son was returning home.

Morning approached swiftly. Though I packed two suitcases with clothes, books, all my "earthly" possessions, I still had leftover items. Some books I could live without, and a graduation present from Nancy, the dentist's daughter, was too large. It was a beautiful portrait of Christ surrounded with a grayish-white wood frame. I imagine. it is hanging on a wall to this day somewhere in Boise. The landlady could do what she wanted, donate or sell everything.

I forgot one minor detail. How was I going to get home? Boise to Bothell was over five hundred miles and took about eight hours by car. I had no money for an airplane ticket. No money or a train ticket. Not even money for a bus ticket.

There was only one solution – hitchhiking.

Walking down the sidewalk with a suitcase in each hand, I realized perhaps I had placed too many books inside. The first ten blocks felt more like ten miles. At the next corner I stopped, sat on the suitcases to rest.

Reaching into my pocket I checked the financial situation. Fifty cents! At least I wasn't completely broke!

Thoughts kept racing through my mind. It might take days hitchhiking to Seattle,

why not hop a train? I'd never done that before, sounded exciting. No, I didn't know where they were heading; I'd probably end up in New York.

As I moved on, a city bus appeared. I had money…it would at least get me out of the city limits. Waving the bus down, I squeezed my way through the aisle. How nice it was to sit down and relax! Pulling out a map to check my bearings, I saw the future didn't look promising. With over five hundred miles ahead, Seattle seemed a million miles away.

I was not a common hitchhiker, but hitchhiking was the only alternative. All the cars were heading toward town instead of out of town. Then I got lucky. A kid about two years older than me was headed for Ontario, Oregon. Right on course, out of Idaho!

My arms ached again as I walked along the highway, a condition that would persist until I reached home. The constant beating of the summer sun, harder, harder and harder, didn't help conditions. If only I could get a ride with someone heading for Seattle!

After an hour during which I mostly sat on my suitcases, an old beat-up brown Chevrolet stopped several yards down the road, almost going into the ditch as it pulled over.

Reaching for the door, I wondered if this was the right decision. But I really didn't have much choice if I wanted to reach Seattle. The driver must have been about sixty or sixty-five years old, hadn't shaved in several days, his clothes were dirty and he smelled like a river rat. Groceries were scattered along the back seat and floor.

"Where ya going, Kid?"

"A small town about twelve miles northeast of Seattle."

"Well, how about that. I have to go to the veterans' hospital in Tacoma, American Lake, for an operation. That will get you most of the way."

After several miles, I had doubts whether the car or driver would ever make it over the Blue Mountains, much less Tacoma, Washington. His driving made me nervous as he slurped down a bottle of beer.

Realizing the seriousness of the situation, I offered to drive and he consented. He kept talking about how he had been fishing in Idaho, camping along the Riverbanks and in general taking life easy.

Beyond all expectation, we finally reached the Blue Mountains. At the top of the range there was a roadside camp/park. My ride wanted to stop and spend the night.

Since my main objective was Seattle, getting home, I tried talking him out of the idea. But he insisted, so I pulled into the camp.

The old man opened several cans of beans and dumped them in a pan that looked like it hadn't been washed since he had bought or found it in a junkyard.

My appetite soon left me. I could only think about how nice it would be to be home.

I wasn't going to waste any more valuable time with this guy. Grabbing my suitcases, I thanked him for taking me this far, bid him farewell and headed for the main road.

The sky turned black as a thunderstorm formed over the mountains, "This is all I need!" I thought to myself.

Just as fast as the rain poured down, a '55 Mercury sped by, noticed me and slowed down, screeching his tires to a stop.

With the wind and rain battering the windshield, I felt secure for a while in a dry, warm car. I could have been standing drenched and cold in the outside storm.

I couldn't believe it when he said he was traveling to Portland. The drive along the Columbia River took my breath away with its power and beauty.

It was late when we arrived in Portland. Not just late, but dark and rainy also. I had no idea where I was or where the freeway to Seattle was. I walked and walked and walked. My arms grew tired and hunger pains snapped inside my stomach. I sat on the suitcases to rest. Within minutes a car stopped.

He seemed nice, several years older than me. After hearing of my journey so far, he offered his apartment as a place to spend the night. I was tired. Sleeping sounded great, especially under a warm, dry roof.

At night he kept putting his feet and legs on my legs. When I moved my legs, he stopped doing it. I guess he was a light sleeper, maybe. How had we ended up in the same bed?

We were up very early and on our way because of his work schedule. At least now I had my directions straight. The rain had stopped. The suitcases were still heavy. But I was heading north. Washington State was just steps away. I wanted to run, fast, over the 1–5 bridge.

The Columbia River was mighty. Halfway across the bridge I stopped. This was the boundary between Oregon and Washington. The river was calm, so peaceful and vast. Her beauty stretched for miles and miles in both directions. Magnificent! The dark blue water, like a mirror ready to waterski on. Yes, truly majestic!

Cars speeding over the 1–5 bridge jolted me back to reality. I stepped into Washington State.

It was early morning; I sure wanted a cigarette. Of course I had no money. Walking along, I reached desperation. In the ditch were several cigarette butts. I could be choosy. Not one with lipstick on it! I straightened a butt out. It only gave me two puffs, two puffs that made me sick!

I was in Vancouver, Washington, a small town by the river…a small town with little to offer, for now.

Even though I was anxious to get home, thinking about facing everyone and answering all the questions had no appeal.

"Heard you quit school."

"Where have you been al l summer?"

"How much money did you save in Boise?"

A car stopped and so did my thoughts on questions.

At the station, a large truck with a trailer home was being serviced.

"Do you need a ride, son?"

A man and wife were headed for a logging camp in the Cascade Mountains near Duval. To reach the site, they'd have to drive two miles past my hometown.

It was easy to see they were Christians. God had given them a special ministry to miners and loggers throughout the United States. They were devoting their time, money and talents to bring church to unusual places.

As the conversation unraveled, I almost told them about my life. I was silent.

It was great to be in Bothell! I walked up the long driveway. It appeared no one was home. They must be at Lake Roediger, the summer cabin.

My last two hours and thirty-three miles of hitchhiking brought me to the lake.

As I opened the cabin door, Mother's jaw lowered six inches; she was too surprised for words. I kissed her cheek.

There weren't as many questions to answer as I had thought there might be.

Everyone was happy to see me.

Home at last!

But the summer of joy of '65 would not linger. College dropouts were in demand. Something to do about Southeast Asia. Something to do about a place called South Vietnam.

# Chapter 8
# The President Sends a Letter

"Greetings from the President of the United States. You are hereby ordered to report for induction into the Armed Forces of the Unites States of America...

Report date "October 12 1965" my twentieth birthday! The escalation of the Vietnam war had caught me. It hadn't taken long for the draft board to find this college drop-out.

Walking up the long driveway from the mailbox I was not surprised.

The situation in Vietnam was growing intense. Eligible drafters were clamoring to enter colleges and universities for a deferment.

And I had just said "goodbye" to college.

At the Seattle induction center, I had one last glimmer – FAIL the physical!

I was one of many young men stripped to our shorts.

The doctor started listening with his stethoscope. He came to me, listened and moved on quickly.

"Excuse me doctor, did you hear my heart murmur?"

This was my last chance!

The doctor returned, listened once more to my heart, smiled then chuckled "Well, I can barely hear it. You are strong enough for the military"

Passing the physical left no doubt "papers" will be arriving soon.

The thought of death in battle or other ways in Vietnam haunted me day and night. Every day and night young boys were being killed in swampy rice paddies of a country no one knew. Every night South Vietnam was on the evening news Kids were dying. Kids were becoming just "body counts"

And where was South Vietnam anyway?

It was not fair. I had more living to do. I enjoyed life too much. I just couldn't go into the army!

The first place they would ship me was Vietnam. I had to find a way out.

Best way was to appeal to the draft board. Though I had dropped out of college, I was still planning to enter the ministry. Or was I?

All I had to do was re-enroll in college and continue as a ministerial student.

Then I would be deferred from the draft.

Sure, ministerial student, that was almost a joke. No I was not ready to go back to college.

I walked to my favorite place in the woods on the hill. This was where I had often come as a child to play and later as years passed to be alone, to think, to just enjoy nature and reflect on beauty of living things.

And now, all of the sudden the years had jumped from childhood to a young man.

Lying back on the soft, dry evergreen needles, all I saw were branches swaying back and forth.

A familiar sight I didn't want to lose.

There stood the giant evergreen tree I had conquered climbing as a boy. How scared I had been!

And now I was scared again.

The draft! I was perplexed. What should I do? What could I do? What were my options?

"Sledge parties" were starting to form, so I heard.

People who had been drafted would have a party and bring sledge hammer along. A smashed hand or smashed foot would keep anyone out of the military.

I was not that desperate yet. Could someone actually do that to themselves?

Some "draft dodgers" were fleeing to the Canadian border just a few hours north. No that was not a good idea. It was not a good idea; it was only running.

And how long would I have to run?

The more I thought about the unknown future years, the more I realized the armed forces have something more valuable than college or university.

Some lessons and experiences only the military can teach.

During the time I found out if drafted, you could join any branch of the arm forces providing that branch took you into active duty before the date ordered to report to the army.

Perfect! I will join the National Guard or Naval Reserve. May just go on active duty for six months and then reserve meetings. That wouldn't be too bad.

Unfortunately, everyone else in the state of Washington had the same idea. The National Guard had filled its quota for several months in advance.

The Air Force reserve was full, The Marines – oh stay away from them.

The Naval Reserve was full-but they did have a two-year program.

Two years! It sounded like an eternity. But I had to make a decision fast. Vietnam was a hotspot.

May be the Navy would be a good teacher.

# Chapter 9
# Navy Boot Camp

"Fasten your seatbelts" flashed overhead—my first commercial jetliner flight. It would not be my last.

San Diego, California, looked dark, with small bright lights as the airplane prepared to land. Many questions had raced through my mind on the flight from Seattle. The future was one gigantic question mark. A lot of questions and no answers.

Ten days after signing my name and taking the oath, "I do," I found myself read but not so willing, for ten weeks of Navy boot camp training. I had successfully dodged the Army, but not the Navy.

There were about thirty other enlistees boarding the plane at Seattle, San Francisco, and Los Angeles.

As we walked through the San Diego airport terminal, a sailor greeted us and said to "muster" outside. "Muster," my first military term. One I would hear too, too often at boot camp.

Everyone formed three ranks, stood at attention out front and waited for a bus I arrive. An hour passed before a gray Navy bus appeared. It seemed like three Ion hours standing at attention!

"There will be NO TALKING, NO EATING, NO SMOKING or ANYTHING E on the bus."

The driver Crouched like we were responsible for making him work late at night. Maybe he had missed a date with his girl. Maybe he had had a bad fight with his wife. He was mad. He was angry!

Strict discipline "by the book" was difficult to learn at first. Not because I'd new been disciplined, but because military life was new, strange, completely the opposite of civilian life.

After breakfast we were transformed from "civilian" citizen to "military" sailor.

Mustered again, all personal belongings, money, combs, etc., anything in our pockets, had to be placed in a pile in front of us. We could do two things: 1. Mail it home, or 2. Donate it to charity.

Next project, Navy issues.

Everyone lined up to receive new "wardrobes." Navy T-shirts, underwear, socks, belts, dress whites, dress blues, dress shoes, work (combat) boots, navy blue sweater, short sleeve whites (shirts), pea coat, foul weather jacket and we can't leave out the navy-blue scarf and hat Of course you need a sea bag as a suitcase.

Everyone was issued a stencil with last name and serial number imprinted. All articles had to be stenciled with a black marker. There was only ONE place and ONE way to stencil, the Navy way! One item at a time, we stenciled as a group.

The last physical transformation, marching to the barber. Or was it marching to the "barbarian?"

"ONE, TWO, THREE." Just three quick swipes, "buzz, buzz, buzz"—no hair!

Everyone's head looked the same.

We lined up for vaccinations, no, they really were "shots"; not just in one arm, but both arms at the same time! And not just a little needle, a power gun needle filled with many vaccines. Some moved and drew blood.

Finally, we were seaman recruits. Seventy-two recruits of Company 529 living together in a naval barracks. And a company commander who had forgotten the term "father figure."

At first, the sound of John Philip Sousa blaring from the tower speakers of the parade grounds was enjoyable. After ten weeks, sounds of military mar es were not on the top of my chart. The parade grounds transformed into a hot, cement, steaming, mall parking lot.

We marched to breakfast, stood at attention. Marched to chapel, stood at attention. Marched to get our clothes, stood at attention. Marched to get our shots, stood at attention. Marched to lunch, stood at attention Marched toa movie, stood at attention. Marched to dinner, stood at attention. We were always marching, music, music, music, marching and standing at attention. This surprised me for a Navy boot camp. It also surprised my feet.

Marching had its problems for green seaman recruits. First you had to find the right "rhythm" in your feet. Music and rhythms go together. Then you must listen for the "commands." With the commands came "direction." "Right face meant turn right. "Left face" meant turn left. "About face" meant turn around completely and march in the opposite direction.

The problem occurred when seaman recruits didn't know the difference between right and left.

Once my rhythm was off and my boots hit the recruit in front of, me. He turned around immediately and hit me in the stomach. Wow! He sure took that personally! But the most dangerous aspect of marching was when rifles were involved. Ouch! In the beginning, mistakes were made, heads were hit, heads ducked and tempers flared.

Every night was wash clothes night. Each article of clothing had to be was spotless by hand with a scrub brush. The white hats and underwear had to be especially clean and white. A large cement table outside the barracks was the work Toward the end of training laundry service was provided.

Since living quarters were limited onboard ship, each piece of clothing had a specific way to be folded and placed in the small "apple box" locker. Our CC (company commander) demonstrated each morning the proper technique. Everyone to practice until they did it right. It had to be the Navy way. Locker inspections decided who needed more instruction.

Personnel inspections were held each morning in our assigned area. Frequently the CC (actually he was a chief petty officer) would review the group before the inspection team arrived. On one occasion, he approached me from behind and yanked three long hairs from the very bottom of my neck. No sane person would think of shaving so low to the chest.

"What is this?" he growled, speaking an inch from my face, holding the hairs in his fingers.

"It's a hair."

"It's a hair what!"

"It's a hair, SIR!"

"Do you know how many days growth that is?"

"Two, SIR!"

"AT LEAST THREE WEEKS!"

"Yes, SIR!"

I hated personal inspections!

"Fire and security" watches were another area in preparation for Navy life. seaman recruit walked inside the barracks at night in a circular path. And another was outside guarding the entrance and clothesline. If anyone approached the command was: "Halt! Who goes there?" Everyone slept well at night knowing our clothes were safe! The hardest part about the outside watch was the enticing view of done town San Diego. You could almost hear, "Come on sailor, go to town and live a little."

Mail call was especially happy and important during boot camp. It made the isolation and military discipline less significant. Mother sent a letter one day telling of an upcoming major operation. I was concerned and wanted so much to talk with her.

At this time in boot camp training, telephone calls were against regulations u you had an emergency or "bona fide" reason. Certainly, I was eligible to call home!

When I reached the CC's office, a sign was tacked on the door.

Knock here hard three times.

(Beneath it was a large, black, circular ink blot.)

Enter – stand at attention.

State your name, rank and service number.

State your business.

I knocked on the door three times.

"I CAN'T HEAR YOU!" roared from inside.

That really rubbed me the wrong way. I banged on the knock spot so hard I thought I had broken a knuckle.

"ENTER!"

Entering, I stood at attention. He wasn't going to catch me doing anything wrong. On the wall, my eyes quickly glanced at a picture of a young girl cut out of a magazine. Underneath the picture read "look spot" and another black dot. I have always looked at people straight in the eyes when I speak to them. The company commander quickly informed me, not so politely, that I wasn't looking at the "look spot."

"Is she smiling at you?" he blurted out.

Straining my eyes, I couldn't see exactly what the expression was on her face.

"I don't know."

"YOU DON'T KNOW WHAT?"

Whoops! There I went again. I just couldn't remember this "Sir" business. "I DON'T KNOW, SIR!"

The next part was easy, no reason to goof up.

"Olson, seaman recruit, 920-43-98. Mother is having major operation in the hospital. Request permission to call home. SIR!"

He sat silent for a moment, not responding.

"Maybe it's best you don't find out how your mother is. My mother was in a hospital for six months once and I didn't always know how she was. Permission denied."

Leaving the office, I felt I had just acquired a "military enemy number one." That was the most ridiculous thing I had ever heard.

After brooding for several days and receiving no mail from home, I decided to ask for a telephone pass once again.

I went through the usual ritual of seeing the company commander. He looked up surprised, bewildered.

"Didn't I let you call home when you heard your mother was going into the hospital?"

That did it! It was all I could do to hide and control the thoughts, emotions and regretful words that almost slipped out. After the pass was signed, I raced to the telephone booths.

Before I could dial, I stopped. What if something was critical? Did I want to know? Of course, I did.

"Dad! It's me!"

Hearing my father's voice, I almost cried from excitement. It seemed so long since I had heard it.

"How's Mom?"

"She's just fine; came home from the hospital tonight."

I slept well! that night. My mother was alright.

The last days of boot camp dragged. However, for once everyone was starting shape into a militant group. Few people stepped on each other while marching ranks. "Right face," "left face," "about face" had no casualties.

Class instruction and training intensified after several weeks.

I had never realized there were so many knots to tie in the Navy. And I had n realized some could be so difficult to master.

The swimming session was easy, but not for some. Everyone had to jump the diving board whether they could swim or not. Instructors stood along the pool with long wooden poles, jabbing those recruits not surfacing and pulling them out Panicked hands grasped for survival.

Everyone jumped in with clothes on. Not as a celebration, but as a lesson staying afloat for days. Making air pockets out of bellbottoms and your shirt could be useful in the future.

The thought of fire at sea onboard a ship always made me wonder—where would you run?

The fire-fighting school was preparation for fighting onboard fires. Beside basics of hose connection and putting out simulated controlled fires, gas mask techniques were given.

Each sailor wearing gas masks would crawl into a fire-and-smoke-filled compartment identical to a ship. Once they were inside the fire-fighting instructor would command, "Take off your gas masks and stand up."

After about thirty seconds he asked, "Where is all the smoke?"

Where was all the smoke? This instructor had one BIG sense of humor.

Often a recruit served as an example to the entire company. Returning from exchange store one day, a "privilege" granted after eight weeks of training, two sailors had candy bars. Candy, aftershave lotion, cologne, etc., were strictly forbidden to purchase. The company commander stuffed two candy bars in each recruit's mouth—paper and all.

Another time he made a recruit eat a pack of cigarettes for smoking on watch.

After a barracks inspection one morning, I also became an "example." Haphazardly, I had left my locker unlocked, a demerit of several points. "Olson, step up on the stairway!"

Oh no, what had I done this time?

"Do you have your key on you?"

Why did he ask me that? We kept our keys and I.I. tags on a metal chain around our necks. To be honest, I wasn't sure whether or not I had the keys.

"I think so, SIR!"


"YOU THINK SO?"


Now he had me trapped. I must say either yes or no. "Yes, SIR, I do!"

"Well, you sure don't have to use it! DO YOU KNOW WHY?"

"No, SIR!"


"BECAUSE YOUR LOCKER IS UNLOCKED, THAT'S WHY! YOU WERE THE ONLY REASON WE FLUNKED OUR INSPECTION!"


He didn't have to kick me in the seat of the pants. I couldn't feel a thing— only humiliation.

The daily class on boating made everyone tense and extremely home sick. The open-air pier was located beneath the paths of jets taking off and landing from the San Diego International Airport. I watched with envy every plane zooming overhead. Only one thought occupied my mind…someday, someday I would be on a similar plane heading home. Naval training would finally be over.

Everyone said boot camp would be the roughest part of the military. They were right almost. Standing in line to receive my orders and travel pay, I knew that two lines were all that separated me from home. I made it successfully— no longer an Sr (seaman recruit), but now an SA (seaman apprentice). Boot camp was a good teacher.

My orders authorized ten days leave before reporting onboard the 55 Tioga County (LST-1158). It carried troops, tanks, jeeps, trucks and ammunition, etc. Having a flat bottom enabled her to go right up on the sandy beaches an, unload cargo. The bow doors opened, a ramp came down, and the vehicles, etc., drove out on dry land. She served with the amphibious force of the Navy. Anyway, that's what I read in a book.

Before leaving San Diego, I asked around at the YMCA if anyone knew the where- abouts of the Tioga (the nickname of Tioga County). Two sailors said they had seen her in South Vietnam waters. South Vietnam waters! Not exactly what I had in mind. Glancing over my shoulder at take-off, I couldn't help but think about the new recruits below. It was rough. But I had become a different person, a stronger, more disciplined person. And the experiences of boot camp would benefit me even after many years following Navy life. I was reminded of sitting in the woods when I received my draft notice.

These weeks were something NEVER taught in college or universities.

I waved to the "poor souls" below having a lecture on boating. It was hard to believe I was actually "in the air." Then my mind returned to more serious thoughts South Vietnam.

All during the flight home I did two things: relished in new freedom and to God.

Wearing a big grin, Dad was at the terminal to welcome me home. I hugged him hard, harder and harder. Walking down the long SeaTac air terminal arm-I was the closest I had ever felt to Dad. It was a great feeling.

I still wasn't used to the bellbottom pants and bulky wool navy-blue uniform of a sailor. But I didn't feel like a sailor at all. No, I was a son. just a son walking w a father that loved me. And I loved him.

Stopping at the airport restaurant I realized something was wrong. There long line. I didn't have to stand at attention or say "Yes, SIR!" or "No, SIR!" The waitress even smiled at me like I was a human being.

Both of us took turns talking. Dad told of new foster brothers in the boys' plans of remodeling the old house, changing the new house, of all the good and news. I rambled on about becoming a sailor. I talked about my orders, my ship, mostly about how wonderful it was being home.

Mom was still recuperating from her operation when I walked into the room. was thrilled to see me. I put my arms around her, hugging tight; I never stop. I never wanted to leave home again NEVER!

# Chapter 10
# Ship is Found

I placed the sea bag on the scale. It was hard to believe the plan to San Diego was ready for departure. My precious two-week leave had sailed like two hours

The flight down was no holiday excursion. Questions mounted into anxiety Where was my ship docked? Was she in South Vietnam? Why was I reporting to San Diego?

Arriving a day early, I rented a room at the YMCA. Checking the registry, I noticed a name followed by "address, USS Tioga County LST-1 158." Knocking on the door, I rechecked the number to make sure it was right a sleepy-eyed Filipino opened the door.

"Are you waiting for the Tioga County?"

"Yes, I am."

He had such a strong, sharp accept, I could barely understand what he said

He preferred to be called "Cap," since his last name was "too long and hard to pronounce."

After traveling together trying to catch our ship, we became close friend and the Tagalog accent disappeared.

Two weeks dragged as Cap and I waited in the San Diego naval transient barracks. A list was read each morning of ships' arrivals and those sailors who would be flown overseas.

Our duty now was cleaning latrines (restrooms) and policing the base we were not "cops" arresting people. This was a Navy term for picking up garbage cans cigarette butts, etc., people had scattered. I had several days of shore petrol duty at the main gate to the officers' golf course. It was so boring saluting. I saluted the car instead of the officers as they arrived and left. But it was better

Finally, the morning arrived when Cap's and my names were announced the USS Tioga County (1158) was overseas. Last report—South Vietnam.

It always felt great calling home. Only this time, I wasn't sure how to tell my parents I was heading overseas and possibly to Vietnam. After several minute of small talk, I built up enough courage.

"Dad, I'm leaving tonight overseas. I'm not sure where my ship is may be Guam, the Philippines, or even South Vietnam."

"Well, Son, we all will be praying for you." How I needed prayers!

The Hawaiian Islands I had never been to Hawaii. The list had started for "join the Navy and see the world" places. My world was growing larger.

Looking out the airplane window I saw Diamond Head was breathtaking. the numerous hotels cluttering Waikiki Beach along coral waters were so small, unreal

Most of the passengers on the flight from San Diego to Honolulu were dependents of military personnel. I saw only one other uniform.

The layover was going to be short. At least I could say, "Sure, I've been to Hawaii." I wondered what I could do.

My dream world was interrupted and turned to gloom as I stepped down the ladder.

There to greet me was a Naval officer.

"You are one of the few active-duty personnel on this flight. You are going to have to stand a guard watch."

He pointed to a hatch underneath the airplane.
"Inside that hatch are some white bags. No one, positively no one, is to remove them. After an hour, another sailor will relieve you. We plan to be here only wo hours. Here's a gun; use it if you have to."

Just great! Beautiful Hawaii and I had to stand guard with a.45 revolver. And a Colt.45 I had never fired! Just what was in those bags?

I didn't have to shoot anyone in Honolulu, but my "Hawaiian vacation" fizzled. Next stop with "Join the Navy and see the world" was Guam, Marianas Islands. I didn't know much about Guam, except what I had seen on TV as a boy, "Victory at Sea" and World War II commentaries. For the Vietnam War, Guam was the base for B-52's bombing North Vietnam.

Arriving at Anderson Air Force Base, I was surprised the MPs wore tropical shorts and jungle-type safari hats. Another surprise was at the Navy check-in desk! There stood a sailor from Bothell High School. I couldn't believe it!

74

We talked about the "good old days back home," how everyone was doing and how different Guam was compared to the great, green, Pacific Northwest. Then his voice softened, almost to a whisper.

"The hardest thing about this job is seeing the arrival and departure of wooden caskets draped with American flags day, after day, after day."

From Anderson Air Force Base all the sailors boarded a Navy bus to the naval station at Guam. Did I see the USS Tioga County? No. Yes, another transient barracks!

This time, I would not have to "police" the base picking up garbage and cigarette butts.

In the barracks I had an all-night "fire and security watch" from 10:30 at night until 6:00 in the morning. I would answer the telephone in the office, check in any late arrivals, walk around the barracks every hour checking for fires, and then telephone a report to the duty officer.

It was monotonous. But the boredom ceased momentarily by an unexpected friend. This friend was a lizard living behind the large oval clock. Patiently waiting for a snack, he/she would slowly creep out and "zap," goodbye fly.

Soon even that was boring. To occupy my mind I started writing poetry Nothing fantastic, just thoughts. Just to pass time. But strangely, "nothing fantastic can turn out to be fairly good.

On Guam, I met one of Cap's friends from the Philippine Navy. He was quick to give me advice about the Navy.

First, you have to get a real long tattoo, maybe a snake or a knife that runs all the way up and down your arm. This makes you look tough. Also, if ever there's a long line, crowd up front, push anyone out of your way. You have to be tough! I restrained myself from laughing. He meant well.

Tom Jones met me at the Navy canteen. Well, he was in the jukebox!

The old hometown looks the same.

As I step down from the plane.

And there to meet me is my mamma and poppa.

It's good to touch the green, green grass of home

What a homesick song, "The Green, Green Grass of Home!"

The dry grass of Guam could not compare to the green grass of the Pacific Northwest!

After several weeks on Guam in transient barracks, the *Tioga County* never arrived. Latest rumor?

"In dry dock, Philippines."

Next stop with "join the Navy and see the world" were the Philippine Islands.

Clark Air Force Base, Philippine Islands, was jammed with military personnel in the terminal. Some arriving, some departing, but mostly army in full battle gear.

After waiting five hours for a Navy bus to arrive, we climbed on board and headed across the island to Subic Bay Naval Base. The hours driving through numerous villages and farmlands opened my eyes and heart to sights unbelievable. It was all foreign to me. And I was the foreigner.

Outside the base's main gate there seemed a lot of activity for six o' cock in the morning. What was it? A carnival? That was my first reaction to the brightly colored, flag-flying jeepneys. Jeepneys were jeeps with benches in the back serving as open air taxis. The outside was colored bright red, yellow, pink and purple, etc., anything to dash it up. There was no carnival, just Filipinos coming to work at the base.

Ahead of the bus I noticed a policeman. Or was it a policeman? Why was he carrying a rifle along with a revolver? Cap pointed out the history of the Huks. They were guerilla soldiers, predominant in this area, who were trying to overthrow the government. The policemen had to be extra careful and always on the lookout for the Huks.

As dawn approached, I noticed several rabbit huts built on over-six-foot poles. Glancing closer, I saw people were living in the shacks! It surprised me. People, families were actually living, sleeping and eating in those grass-covered huts. Everyone, myself included, stood on the edge of their seats. This was the Philippines!

Passing an ox-drawn cart, the bus almost forced it off the road. A man was in a muddy pond washing his water buffalo. Children, some dressed, others naked, lined the road whenever the bus passed through a village. They all had smiles. They all waved their hands making a V for "victory" with their fingers.

"Hi-ya, Joe! Hi-ya, Joe!"

The greeting would become familiar along with "Coins, Say-loor, coins?"

We passed acres of wheat or hay, with several water buffalo and Filipinos working in the fields.

"Hey, Cap, a kid is sleeping on top of that water buffalo!"

*How strange,* I thought. The water buffalo was plowing away, and there's a little Filipino boy fast asleep. Cap was sitting behind me. His face leaned against the bus window. I turned around.

Without looking up, gazing out, he mumbled, "Ya, it's very comfortable."

Looking around, I saw everyone was just as excited as me. The surroundings were so strange, foreign. But to the Cap, this was home. We were the foreigners. the expression on his face was clear. He had drifted back to his own childhood, when he had dozed off on a water buffalo. And now he was a U.S. sailor. Although still a Filipino national, he had been chosen and trained to be a steward. His duties would be to cook and serve U.S. Naval officers plus clean and manage their living quarters He had come a long way. He had seen and accomplished things many young Filipinos only dream about.

Most ships operating in South Vietnam, the South China Sea or the Gulf of Tonkin generally stopped at Subic Bay naval station for supplies, repairs and "liberty call."

The transient barracks at Subic were just transient barracks. By now I was getting sick of trying to catch my ship and all the waiting around. At least I had a chance for some liberty call.

Olongapo City, Zambales, was a small town with only a bridge separating it from the base. Sewage smell reeked from the river as I crossed over. The water looked murky brown, dirty and contaminated. My attention soon focused on small children swimming below.

"Coins, Say-loor! Coins! Coins!" Of course, I had coins.

Diving from their small wooden boat, they made sure not one coin was missed.

As I reached the other side of the bridge, a loudspeaker blared, "Change American dollars into pesos HERE!"

Sailors were warned not to change money except at the "official" stand something about "sleight of hand," "fast money shuffle" and other "schemes" to short change" unsuspecting sailors.

I was amazed to find about twenty jeepneys lined up one after the other each driver yelling to hire them. It did look like a carnival!

It was obvious the town environment was suited for one purpose —the American sailor and fulfillment of his sexual desires. The main road consisted of bar, bar, bar, bar, hotel, bar, bar, bar, bar and on and on. Once in a while there was a restaurant The sidewalks were covered with small cart stands of cigarettes, gum, fruits (melons, papayas), peanuts, popcorn and oh yes, barbecued "monkey meat" on a sick. delicacy was rumored to be dog meat Cap and I went to a restaurant in Olongapo. It was the best rice I had ever the creme sauce made it special. As I left the restaurant, I had to find out what ingredients were in the sauce.

"Pig's blood," smiled Cap.

The reek of sewage made it difficult to breathe at first. But eventually they became unrecognizable.

Small Filipino boys were quick to offer services.

"Want shoeshine, Say-loor?"

"How much is it?"

"Whatever you want to tip me."

That didn't sound too bad. As I leaned against the building, it wasn't long before four little Filipino boys were working vigorously on the shoes. As it turned out "tip" for a shine proved costly. A tip for the boy who did the shining, a tip for the boy with the polish, a tip for the boy who supplied the rags, and lastly, a tip for the one who supplied the stool for the shoes to rest on.

With my soft heart, it was hard not to give money to every child that asked "coins?" But I soon found out it didn't take long to become broke. I always wondered what the kids did with their money. Once a small boy said he needed "coins" to eat. Instead of giving him money, I invited him to eat at a restaurant. We had a great time. He was proud to be eating with a U.S. sailor. And I was proud to be eating with a hungry boy.

Some children would lead their blind mother, father, or grandparents through the streets with outstretched hands waving, quivering, hoping to feel money.

The most pitiful sight in all my travels to South east Asia happened in Olongapo. Heading for the main gate, I came upon a cripple. His withered legs were wrapped together with dirty old rags. The rags extended around his feet then around his neck. His body made the shape of a semicircle. He walked on his hands using a pai of thongs. I tried not looking, but I couldn't help it. I will never forget him. As I passed, he smiled. He smiled at me.

Six long months of transient barracks and I finally caught up with the Tioga County. As she pulled into the harbor, my first reaction was, "That's not a ship! It's a barge!"

The "Tiger" (ship's nickname) was coming back from operating off the coast of Vietnam. Whenever an LST beached, she had to drop her stern (rear) anchor. the ship sailed right up on the beach. In her last beaching, the Tiger's screws (propellers) had been tangled up with the anchor cable. She had had to sail to Subic Bay Naval station for repairs. I was happy!

When I reported on board, the Tioga County was in dry dock. There was no water under the ship. To the right was the longest and steepest ladder I had ever seen. how was I going to climb up with my sea bag without running out of breath or stumbling? I made it to the top without incident.

As a seaman apprentice with no specialty, I was placed in deck force. Soon every morning I would be jolted out of the rack (bed) with a sound you could not hide from.

"Now, sweepers, Sweepers! Man, your brooms! Give the ship a clean sweep down fore and aft. Now, sweepers, Sweepers!"

It wouldn't have been so bad if all we had to do was sweep. But we had to mop the deck also. And an LST's deck was large, large enough for a helicopter to land on, carefully, and for tanks and trucks to beach.

There was something unique about the vastness, smell, color, motion and beauty of the ocean that left a person in awe. But then she could be just the opposite—wild, cruel and destructive.

Part of deck force's responsibility was to stand watches day and night. There were various "lookout" positions on the ship. Any lights observed had to be reported by headset phone to the boatswain mate on duty. During the night in the middle of the ocean, the blackness of the water actually made the horizon appear a light gray but it grew monotonous just looking and searching.

We always knew when Vietnam beaches were close. The constant flare for miles in all directions, lit up the beach.

During night watches, because of the total darkness and loneliness I made up "memory games." Sometimes I would try hard to go back in my mind as far as my memory could travel—once as a baby, but usually first as a small toddler. I was surprised. Other times I would recall being in elementary school, or junior high or high school. I could look back and "picture" all the girls I had known. It was nice to relive the "dates" and girlfriends I had known.

Although not with total recall, I'd sing in my mind the hymns I had learned in church. Usually then I would "revisit" the many church services I had attended Over the hours playing "memory games," I became less bored and more conscious of my life. They were exercises.

Besides standing watches, deck force personnel also had to steer the ship.

The flat bottom enabling the ship to beach was also responsible for throwing us around in rough seas.

When you "relieve the helm" the sailor steering tells you the course and how much adjustment needs to be taken left or right rudder. It's not like a car so you might have to turn the wheel ten degrees left rudder and watch to a certain point where the needle goes on the course and then swing back to ten degrees right rudder.

Naturally, the rougher the water the more adjustments you have to make what a time to first steer the ship!

"Request permission to relieve the helm, SIR! Steering course two, niner zero checking course. Permission granted."

I grabbed the wheel as the ship rocked, rolled and swayed back and forth were falling off the quartermaster's desk. I had trouble keeping my balance let alone steer the ship.

"MIND YOUR HELM!" shouted the officer of the deck.

"Mind your helm? What did he mean by that?" I quickly asked the boatswain-mate of the watch.

"It means you have drifted too far off course. Answer back, 'Mind my helm aye, SIR!' then get back on course as soon as possible."

Next day the sea was glassy smooth, dark blue and calm. How much easier it was to control the ship and stay right on course!

In the middle of the Pacific Ocean, I found on the deck a small dead bird he hadn't made the flight. A song I sang in church as a youth came to my mind:

*Why do you let the troubles*
*of tomorrow bring sorrow to*
*your heart and burdens too?*
*For if the Father's eye is*
*on the sparrow, then surely*
*He will take care for you.*

I asked God, "What happened here?"

Painting the ship occurred a little here and a little there, usually whenever rust appeared. It was one job nobody liked. First the rusted paint had to be chipped. of chipping hammers were thrown overboard as an excuse to walk back to the room for another one.

One day, I had to paint the ship. This was no ordinary paint assignment. to paint near the top of a smoke stack. In order to do this, I had to sit on a ladder, which was just a regular swing. After being hoisted to the top, I realized difficulties involved. The ship was swaying back and forth. I could chip the rust short time before the ladder would swing out. When the ladder came back closer to the smokestack I would chip again.

The waters never calmed and I kept swinging back and forth. Then the ride was interrupted.

"Hey Olson, can you type?"

I thought for just a second. I could type fifty words a minute in the 9th grade, but I had to peek a little at the keys, well, a lot at the keys! Why was I debating the issue?

"Sure, I can type!" I answered.

"Come on down!"

This was the beginning of yeoman/personnel man (YN/PN) Olson. No deck force. No more "Sweepers, Sweepers." No more night watches. No more ping paint.

Now it was the ship's office! Typing entries into crew's records, publishing daily POD (Plan of the Day), and when in port, going to the naval stations to pick up mail.

Once at Da Nang, I was walking to the base for mail and a Vietnamese solider on a motorcycle offered a ride. He noticed my empty mailbag. When we passed main gate and through a small village, I became concerned. Where was he taking me? Did he think I had important documents, maybe top secret?

Actually, he was taking a shortcut to the side entrance of the base.

The best job was sorting the mail and having "Mail call, ship's office" broadcast throughout the ship.

How nice to have a ship's office of only four sailors! With two white sailor and two black sailors, the staff was very salt and pepper. One black sailor was like a true brother. The other one thought his back was stabbed every time he turned around simply because he was black. I soon ignored it. But I couldn't ignore his constant record of playing Aretha Franklin. Months and months of the same song!

For once, I thought, maybe the Navy isn't all that bad.

The summer of '67 was an active one for our ship. There was a lot of beaching along the Vietnamese coast, "operation double eagle" being the largest and Chu lie being the scariest—Viet Cong snipers firing at the crew.

The ship was escorted and helped move thirty gunboats "monitors' from river assault squadron up the Saigon River.

When we arrived at Vung Tao the bay was crowded with ships at anchor. We thought we would head for the Philippines since a generator was having problems. Other ships must have been worse off. A cheer went throughout the ship when it was announced we'd be loading up the next day and sailing up the Saigon River.

When in port it was easy to get mail. Out at sea it was more difficult the fleet post office knew nothing at times of our whereabouts. Frequently, the crew had no mail.

A helicopter would sometimes drop mail bags on the deck. And sometimes we would have to "fish" the bags out of the water.

At Vung Tao, I received a "special letter" from my eleven-month-younger sister, Pat. It was addressed, "Mr. Gene Olson and guest." At first, I laughed, "and guest," then I wanted to cry. Of all the weddings I wanted to attend, this would be the most important. And here I was stuck on a ship in South Vietnam! Stupid Vietnam

The next two days helped me forget the "wedding" as the ship prepared for going up the river. Thousands of C-rations and loads and loads of ammunition were brought onboard. Two large Conex boxes, steel containers, were placed on slanted ramps. By a human chain, we passed sandbags to line the Conex boxes and also around the numerous machinegun positions.

From the pier, white phosphorous cylinders had to be carried by hand and placed in the Conex boxes. The boxes were placed on ramps in case we were fired at or there was a fire. Chains would be released and the boxes would slide overboard in the river. White phosphorous could burn through even the ships steel.

A portable morgue was lowered to the tank deck. It had space for five bodies. When that was full, the walk-in cooler at mess deck would be used.

The crew worked in the evening and all through the night. Everyone was dirty and covered with sand. The captain came out telling everyone they had done a good job, and then started pouring "shots" of whiskey in paper cups for the crew No one could shower since the muddy river water would clog up the evaporators, etc.

The last cargo was the Ninth Infantry division. The three hundred troops outnumbered the one hundred fifty crew members. We had a special compartment for soldiers, but it had never been used, yet.

After being anchored at the mouth of the Saigon River, the thirty gunboats from River Assault Squadron arrived. They would give the Tioga an escort while it moved to a new location.

There was no trouble going up the Saigon River. There was a lot of black smoke in the distance, but that was all. However, I'm still searching for the videos from the person filming a circling helicopter.

In the evening, the Tioga beached at Dong Tam, an army base. It was here I saw my first USO show. The three girls singing and dancing were very beautiful and yes very sexy. There were "round eyes" in the world after all!

I always watched Jonathan Winters on TV. To see him in person in Vietnam was great. When artillery started zinging over the crowd, Jonathan Winters said, glad those are going out and not coming in."

Later in the summer, again at the mouth of the Saigon River, a helicopter a celebrity to visit the ship and crew. The Untouchables made Robert Stack a star. When the boatswain's pipe sounded, the word was passed throughout „ Elliot Ness, arriving."

A petty officer from the ship's office was going to present a "welcome aboard kit to Robert Stack during ceremonies at the crew's mess hall. At the last minute he changed his mind. No one wanted to do it. I was the last hope and said, yes.

While I stood next to Robert Stack, a Polaroid picture was taken. After thirty-five years the color has faded some and scratches have appeared, but there I am.

From Dong Tam the Tiger headed to the Rat Sang Special Zone and anchored on the Song Soirap River of the Mekong Delta. The Army base at Nha Be was close the ship.

Instead of a "taxi service" the Tioga County was the "Mekong Hilton" for the Ninth Infantry division. Bravo Company would leave the ship on search and destroy missions. When they returned, Charlie Company would go out on search and destroy missions. There was a break so the troops could relax, eat good Navy food (steak and eggs for breakfast) and sleep more comfortably between missions.

While in ship's office, I had no watches. But while we were anchored on the river, I had a watch on the front of the ship. I was issued a pair of binoculars, headphones to the pilot house, a rifle and bullet clips. I was not to load the rifle unless permission was granted from the pilot house. And of course, no firing unless fired at first All movement to and around the ship had to be reported to the pilot house, also any movement along the riverbanks.

This particular day was my younger sister's wedding. Oh, how I wanted to be there! Anger had been growing since I had received the invitation. Depression and self-pity were taking control. I was miserable!

That the scorching sun had blistered my lips didn't help the situation. Then something approached the ship. It had an outboard motor with one operator.

As the small boat came closer, I was able to see more and report it to the pilot house.

"There is a green tarp wrapped around a body only thing visible is a pair of muddy boots."

I stopped. I wondered. How many people would be affected by his death? Maybe a mother, a father, brothers, sisters, relatives? Or maybe a wife, sons, daughters, a girlfriend?

The more I thought about this dead soldier, a stranger to me, the more my sister's wedding became insignificant. I was alive!

"There's a helicopter coming in."

Another "killed in action."

Later in the ship's office, a soldier came to the door.

"Can I borrow your typewriter? I need to type out a death report."

His eyes became a little watery. Then he told me about one of his buddies. His friend had been preparing a death report on a close friend. Before finishing he had gone "berserk."

"If a friend of mine was killed, I'd refuse to type the death report," he told me. If a friend of mine was killed, I didn't know what I would do.

# Chapter 11
# Okinawa and Office of Naval Intelligence (ONI)

It was a calm, pleasant evening as the Tioga was tied up on the pier in Okinawa. A warm breeze blew over the naval base. Okinawa had a busy naval port to load supplies, support vehicles, machinery and troops up rivers and along the coast of South Vietnam. As usual, ship's movements were kept secret.

Naha was a small, interesting city. I walked around taking photographs of children, buildings and even a storefront mannequin of a wedding couple. Soon I was "barhopping" and meeting sailors from the ship. fearing the point of "I've had too much to drink," I headed back to the Tioga.

I had always enjoyed meeting new people, especially those I didn't well. A sailor I didn't know walked back to the ship with me. Well, I knew he worked in the engine room. I couldn't see anything strange in his request that we go to the fantail (rear of the ship) and talk.

We sat down and talked a while, small talk. It was still very dark, not a single person was around. He put his arm around me and held my wrist with his other hand.

"Olson, I want to have sex with you."

"What?"

"I want to have sex with you."

"You must be drunk!"

"No, I'm not."

I got up, but he held me back with both his arms. Wanting to fight back, I compared his size to mine and realized that was senseless. The only solution would be to talk him out of it, or a quick, surprise move.

"Look, you let me go and I'll forget everything. If you don't, tomorrow I'm going straight to the captain."

"You go to the captain and I'll tell him it was your idea."

What if he did say I had wanted to have sex with him? It would be my word against his. Three decks up I heard footsteps. I screamed out; immediately he forced his hand over my mouth and nose. I couldn't breathe! He kept on saying how much he needed me, wanted me, wanted to have sex. At this point I knew he was not drunk, maybe a little high, but he realized what he was saying. Yet, I still found it hard to believe!

What could I do? God help me! Suddenly I made a quick, surprise move, escaping from his strong grip. Though it was dark, I ran. I ran where crew members would be—the mess deck, a place where sailors ate, played cards, wrote letters I watched evening movies, etc.

I sat at a table; my heartbeat thumped faster and faster. I thought about what had just happened—or what might have happened. Then he appeared, climbing down the ship's ladder. Sitting across from me, he whispered only one sentence, better not tell anyone what I tried to do."

I convinced myself the next day that nothing had actually happened, my ship-mate had been drunk. But during dinner, he sat across from me at the same table. The tables were very small, just big enough to hold four Navy food trays. Seeing his face, especially his eyes, I wanted to run, hide, be alone.

The next liberty call, at least I was off the ship, a nice relief.

After drinking myself "silly," I walked into a bar and noticed a table full of chief petty officers from the ship. These guys were truly "old salts" of the Navy.

We talked and I drank their free beer, talked and drank beer, talked an drank. One petty officer was a friend and we talked frequently on the ship.

"Olson, I know you haven't been in the Navy very long. If there is ever anything bothering you about the Navy, feel free to talk with me about it. I have been in for a lot more years than you. Maybe you have some questions or something on your mind."

If only he knew what was on my mind! I could not be on the same ship as my "friend."

After I told the chief petty officer about the incident, he asked, "Will you say those exact words to the executive officer?"

I hated to talk about it, but I agreed. The next day I spoke to the X.O.

"There will be some civilian investigators coming aboard this afternoon to ask you a few questions. Will you answer them?"

"Yes, Sir, I will."

What else could I say, "No, Sir, I won't! I want to forget everything. Just get me off this ship!"

Instantly I could tell who they were as they boarded the ship – civilian clothes, suits, both carrying briefcases. My heart started thumping again!

Soon the boatswain mate blared over the ship's intercom, "Now hear this Seaman Olson lay (report) to the executive officer's stateroom."

I'd never been there before.

"These two men are agents from the Office of Naval Intelligence. They are here bask you a few questions."

Each agent held a pencil and tablet in his hand.

"First of all, we want to inform you of your rights under the Uniform Code of Military justice. You don't have to answer any questions if you feel it can be used against you in a court martial."

COURT MARTIAL! I hadn't done anything wrong. Why did they have to say?

As I talked, they took brief notes.

Later I was informed by the ONI agents we were both needed for further questioning. We would have to go to their headquarters at the Naha Naval Base. Sitting in the car, no one spoke. When we arrived at ONI offices, they placed us in separate small rooms.

My rights under the UCMJ were repeated. Then the questions started to pour each agent taking turns firing, then writing notes on their tablets.

"How long have you known him?"

"When did you first meet him?"

"Have you ever engaged in any homosexual acts?"

Back onboard ship, I was relieved everything was over. But it was just the beginning. The X.O. informed me ONI wanted to keep me on the base for further questioning. In one hour, my ship was getting underway for the Saigon River. I wanted to be on her when she reached Saigon. It was the only time we had been given notice.

As I packed my sea bag, everyone had to ask questions.

"Hey Olson, why are you packing your sea bag?"

"Where are you going?"

"Why did you leave the ship with those guys?"

There was only one answer for all the questions, "I can't talk about it."

We went over similar questions back at Office of Naval Intelligence headquarters. One agent left the room and returned later with a Polaroid camera. They wanted a picture of the scratches on my face caused by me breaking away from the sailor I had never noticed them before.

Leaving the office, I felt like a nervous wreck— all those questions! Did they believe me? I wanted to run, but where? Where could I run on the tiny island of Okinawa? There was no place to go. The sight of a sailor made me sick, even I was a sailor.

When I reported to the transient barracks, the master-at-arms was not present so went into the Quonset hut. The sailor next to me asked why I was there, "Getting discharged, separated, going on to another duty station, what?"

"I can't talk about it."

Why not? I needed someone to talk to, someone that knew something about the Navy. When I repeated my predicament to him, he was quick to give free advice.

"Do you want out of the Navy? Just tell them you want out and you'll be out. They'll probably have a big investigation on both of your backgrounds."

Oh great! What was going on back home? Had they already started to ask questions? Why had they made me leave the ship anyway? Didn't they believe me?

I was summoned to the master-at-arms' office; a rough-looking sailor first class petty officer, sat at a crude desk.

I turned to my orders. "OFFICE OF NAVAL INTELLIGENCE INVESTIGATION" stuck out worse than a sore thumb.

"Olson, I don't know why you are here. But don't give us any trouble and we won't give you any."

What possessed him to say that? I hadn't done anything wrong! I hadn't caused any trouble!

Leaving the office, I sat down along a ditch bank in front of the huts.

Loneliness and I guess doubt about what we're happening or would follow in the next few days dragged me into deep depression. If only there was one, just one person I could talk to. Then thoughts of home raced through my mind. I could walk the streets, of Bothell, play in the woods. My memory was sharp, but nothing took the place of actually being there.

I wondered what everyone was doing. It sure would be great to be home! Thinking more about the investigation, all the questions, and whether or not the ONI agents believed me, sent my mind spinning. Dropping my head into my hands, I started crying. It felt good letting my emotions fly out.

"What's the matter, kid?"

Looking up, I saw the master-at-arms. I told him how I felt, how I never wanted to see a sailor again and how I wished I knew what was happening at ONI. he seemed to understand the situation a little bit. He returned later with a couple of blue pills, sleeping pills, I guess.

Lying in the rack, even with the sleeping pills, I couldn't sleep. I wanted to run, anywhere, just to get away from everyone. But something was keeping me from running. Was it fear? Was it because there was no place to run to? Or, was it cause of a strange Power? A Power that I sensed understood what I was experiencing A Power that had compassion. A Power that wanted to pull me up and help. Oh God! Please help me!

Two days passed. No word from the Office of Naval Intelligence. what was happening?

My time was spent sweeping the streets surrounding our huts, scrubbing walls, ceilings and floors of the restrooms. One day, they sent me out to pick up cans, bottles, sticks and paper out of the gutters. There certainly was no challenge feeling of accomplishment in what I was doing. This made the hours drag even

I wanted desperately to be back on my ship!

Coming back from liberty, drinking in Naha one evening, I felt discouragement creep in again. As usual, I couldn't sleep. Previously I had asked to see a chaplain, someone I could talk to in confidence, to help me try to understand what was happening. All my emotions were building up within.

"The naval chaplain flew to the Philippines last night." Did they have only one chaplain on the base?

I didn't know whether I was going to make it.

Walking along the base fence, for the first time I thought about running A Did they expect me to take this calmly, to act normally? I also thought about the fi day I had been questioned by the ONI agents. Five days had passed without seeing them. What had they done in those five days? This morning they had called me again, asking the same questions over and over. At one point I had broken down cried, cried like a baby. What was taking so long? Why had they told me I might to take a lie detector test? Didn't they believe me? I walked further. I wanted to sit a corner with total isolation and forget, forget everything.

It was growing darker as I walked. by eyes glanced up to see a beautiful white" steeple on a church. Maybe there was a chaplain inside? Both front and back doors were locked. Off to the left was a sign, "Prayer Chapel." Stepping inside, I saw no one was there. Up front was a picture of Jesus Christ. On each side was a candle. I both candles. I let Jesus, the light of the world. It was quiet, peaceful. Placing my hand over my face, I wept...unashamed. Help seemed so far away, and so did my God

I prayed.

If only I could spend the night, right there, all alone, with God. "REVEILLE! REVEILLE!"

How I dreaded this day! What was going to happen this morning? When would I go back to my ship?

"OK, Olson, out of your rack!"

The sailor's grouchiness climaxed it

"I'm not getting up until I've seen a chaplain, a lawyer, or a psychiatrist!"

I threw the covers over my face; I was mad. And I wasn't moving, either, until had seen someone, anyone, to talk to!

The sailor stormed out of the hut. Within minutes he was back.

"Olson, the master-at-arms wants to see you in his office, now!"

Well, I guessed I had better get up. They had said they wouldn't give me any trouble if I didn't give them trouble.

"I've called a chaplain. Get cleaned up, shave and go see him."

It felt good discussing my ordeal of being kicked off my ship and thrown into an ONI investigation. However, when I finished talking, I wasn't getting the help I had thought I would receive. For several minutes we sat still; no one spoke. Total silence. Say something!

"Well, guess I'll be going."

I really didn't want to go. Maybe this would start the conversation rolling

"OK," replied the chaplain, "I have a lot of work to do on tomorrow's sermon"

Thinking about self as usual, I got up to make my exit. I thought he had a lot of nerve putting a sermon before me! Didn't he understand what I was going through? Couldn't he realize I needed help?

As I was walking from the chapel, a thought raced through my mind "You don't feel too good, do you? You're hurt bad. You feel as though you were pushed out the door. Remember this very moment in years to come. When that person, comes to you in search of answers, comfort or strength, and you have so many things to do, remember how you feel right now."

Was it God's voice?

The days started growing worse. I felt I should see a psychiatrist before things became twisted up within my mind until I completely broke down. This attitude brought me walking one night across the street to the naval dispensary. I pounded on the door; no one answered. Just to the right was a bell. I rang it.

"What do you want, Sailor?" "I want to see a psychiatrist." "All the doctors have left."

"Look, Sailor, I want to see a psychiatrist – NOW!"

He opened the screen door. After I filled out a form with my name, rank number and reason for visit, he stamped "EMERGENCY" on it. Now I was getting someplace.

We both got into a car and headed for the Air Force hospital. "Olson, the doctor will see you now."

Once again it felt good speaking with someone about my thoughts and emotion

However, after several minutes I again felt like he had no empathy to the situation nor could he help me.

"Are you a psychiatrist or a medical doctor?" "I'm an M D."

"Well, I want to see a psychiatrist!" services getting motions. situation,

Jumping up, I headed for the door. He couldn't help me. Wait a minute that was pretty rude, to just get up and walk out, even if I was fed up with the military.

Why not give him a chance?

Returning to my seat, I apologized.

"Sorry, Sir. It's just that everything is crushing in on me at once."

He told me he was glad I hadn't left. Most of his patients were dependents oi the base that came to him if they had the slightest sneeze, thinking they were dying After both of us talked further he assured me I was in no need of a psychiatrist Sure, what I had gone through and was now experiencing caused great emotions stress, but he thought I was handling the situation quite remarkably. He wondered what had kept me from running away from the circumstances. I, too, began to wondered Then the doctor told me about the base hospital and how rough, how critical some cases were. Young soldiers from Vietnam who had watched their friends blow up in front of their eyes. Others that had thrown down their rifles on the battlefield saying, "I refuse to fight," and walked away from the conflict.

Suddenly, I felt very small. My problem was nothing compared to others. I wasn't as bad off as I had thought.

Maybe he wasn't a psychiatrist, but he knew people. I left reassured I still had my senses and was handling everything with the right perspective.

Returning to the Quonset hut, I slipped up the hill! to the naval chapel. I was the only one sitting in the hut. There was calmness, a peacefulness I hadn't experience in a long time. I noticed a magazine nearby called His and started reading an artic on the thirteenth psalm. I likened myself to a modern David.

HOW long Wilt thou forget of me, oh Lord forever? how long wilt thou hide thy lace Loom me!


*How considered Shall I take counsel in my soul, having sorrow in my least daily Consider and hear me,0 Lord my God; lighten my eyes I will sink unto the Lord, because he hath dealt bountifully with me.*


Would I ever be able to sing unto the Lord?

GREAT! Packing my sea bag, I found it hard to believe the time had finally, final come for my transfer back to the ship.

At command headquarters I picked up new orders. Since my ship was in Saigon, I was ordered to report to a sister ship also headed to Saigon. I would just "hitchhike up the Saigon River.

Waiting for the Navy taxi, I reminisced on how well everything had turned out.

Many thoughts raced through my mind, but I was now content. The taxi arrived.

Grabbing my sea bag, I reached for the rear door. But wait…there was already a sailor in the back seat. The only sailor I hoped I'd never see again. The ONI agents had said they had given him a lie detector test. Every time he had lied, they had stopped and told him to come back when he was ready to tell the truth. But what was he doing here, now, in my taxi?

Sitting in the taxi, no one spoke a word. No one looked at each other Our orders were identical, we would be hitchhiking on another LST. ft was just like the Navy to do something like this!

When we reported onboard ship, the officer of the day knew nothing of our circumstances. We were assigned temporary berths in the forward troops' compartment. This space was usually used for storage for sea bags and extra crews' personal belongings when troops were not onboard. We were the only ones in the co as we went up the Saigon River everyone was at general quarters. compartment. I compartment were sealed watertight. Since this was not our ship, we did not have an as- signed GQ area. But we could not leave the compartment. No one spoke a word.

I was on my rack one evening, staring at the rack above, thinking, wishing I could catch just a glimpse of the Saigon River. My "friend" was I very top. I was on the bottom.

"Olson, the agents told me not to touch you or I'd be in more trouble than I am in now. I won't force you, but I want you to know I want to have sex with you. You're not a man until you have had sex with a woman, man or animal. Just come over to my rack when you're ready. I'll be waiting for you."

I couldn't believe what I had heard! I was dumbfounded.

The next day my attitude toward him changed, a little.

"Olson, I'm sorry for everything I've done to you. I don't know what; my drives and desires are all mixed up. I hate to be kicked out of the Navy and I'm certainly not going home. Just what am I going to do?"

I think he was sorry.

Our ship was not in Saigon. Within two days the ship headed bac down the Saigon River. Where was the Tioga County? Keelung! Japan seemed halfway around the world at the time.

Going over the South China Sea to Keelung, there almost was a man overboard. The wind was blowing cold rain as we sailed into the Formosan harbor. What a sight! Finally, there she was, my ship!

I was happy to be on board. Everyone was surprised to see me. "Where have you been?"

"What happened?"

"I want to forget everything." I ignored all questions.

Where was my "friend?" He was nowhere in sight. I do know we boarded the ship at the same time. Someone told me the captain transferred him to another ship back in the states. I never did find out what finally happened.

Forty letters and fifteen hometown newspapers were stacked up waiting to be opened. I was so excited I never bothered reading postmarks. What a joy of confusion Though Christmas was long gone, a letter contained special "Christmas greetings from the people of my hometown of Bothell to residents in the armed forces. Twenty-five signatures touched me.

Three days later, word was passed throughout the ship—we're heading home! The only thing the crew could think about was seeing America and Americans once again. It also meant leave. I just couldn't wait to get home! I just couldn't wait to see everyone!

Within thirty days, our ship passed Point Loma through San Diego harbor. Soon I would be on a plane heading for the green and glorious state of Washington. Home at last!

Only one sentence filled my mind as the plane circled over Seattle and Puget Sound, I will sing unto the Lord, because He hath dealt bountifully with me.

Yes, I will sing.

Yes, I will remember.

# Chapter 12
## Leave/Liberty

On leave was glorious! Months at sea, away from America, only shipboard life, then you were going home. You no longer felt like a sailor. The ship was not your home. The military had no control. You were home, a civilian, for a short time. You were back with the real family.

Adjustments to family life, though temporary, could be frustrating. Shipboard meals were, "Pass the fucking bread Pass the f...ing butter!" Every sentence had the word "f...ing." "Please" was not part of a sailor's vocabulary.

Once I almost forgot I wasn't onboard ship. Luckily, my speech improved as I realized I was dining with the Olson family.

What would leave be without walking the streets of Bothell, my hometown? The happy times of years past my bicycle in front of Meredith's Five & Dime, the corner drugstore with genuine cherry cokes and chocolate cokes, and still only one place for a hamburger.

Of course I had to stop in the Bothell State Bank. My childhood bank account with pennies, nickels and dimes deposited weekly had once made me feel rich.

There was something more important in this bank than memories of a childhood savings account. My friend Rich's father still had an insurance company inside. Whenever I came in, if he was with someone, he always raised his hand high in a wave and smiled. If free, he immediately came up to me and we talked.

The talk was always about his son, Rich. His face would glow with pride, admiration and love. I always started the conversation with, "How's Rich?"

"Rich graduated from Washington State University."

"Rich is a helicopter pilot in South Vietnam. He just volunteered for a second tour of duty."

Being a helicopter pilot was more impressive than being a "swabby" sailing up the Saigon River. I think Rich's dad at least thought it was good I had been to Vietnam. The problem with leave was it went so fast and then you must return to Navy life.

When the ship was at homeport, it was not like being underway. There were liberty and weekend passes.

San Diego was a Navy town. Since enlisted personnel couldn't leave the ship in civilian clothes, there were many "stores" with lockers to rent. Usually, a sailor would go directly to his locker to change into civilian clothes. But it was easy to tell the difference between sailors in civilian clothes and civilians in civilian clothes.

It was easy for a sailor's wallet to become empty on liberty. It was even easier to find a loan shark. The owner of the locker store would "lend" out cash at 100 percent interest, five dollars for ten dollars, ten dollars for twenty dollars. The debt was added onto the month's locker fee. Great scam!

Walking alone in downtown San Diego, I saw a bright florescent-lit sign, "LUTHERAN SERVICEMEN CENTER."

Steps led down from the sidewalk to a basement entrance. I entered a large room and to my surprise and enjoyment, two lovely young girls were serving coffee, doughnuts, and smiles.

The one with pearl earrings, the one with straight shoulder-length hair curled under…this was the one I wanted to meet! This was the one I wanted to know!

And I did.

One girl asked, "Do you know how to ride a horse?"

Did I know how to ride a horse? How difficult was it to ride a horse? Anyone could ride a horse.

"Sure, I can ride a horse!"

The friend of my "pearl" girl had two horses. We all would go riding.

"The Singing Hills of El Cajon," an appropriate name, especially to a sailor. The rolling hills were a vast contrast to rolling seas.

Climbing on the horse I had second thoughts—did I really know how to ride a horse? Slowly riding along the trail, I found it was easy. Suddenly the horse to the left took off on a wild gallop and jerked left. My horse decided to take chase, galloping after the other horse at high speed. How did you stop a horse? I kept yelling, "whoa, whoa," but that was useless. I pulled on the reins, to no avail. Finally, one horse stopped and then mine. I haven't been on a horse since!

I was invited to spend the weekend once, both girls were there. Sunday morning everyone went to church. The "pearl" girl and I stayed home. Nice opportunities for a sailor with everyone gone. Rolling around on the carpet was my idea. Rolling the Monopoly dice was her idea! She won!

Memories of the Singing Hills of El Cajon are still songs in my heart. Two young girls sharing friendships…friendships to a sailor. They would never know the kindness, affection, beauty they displayed during my loneliness.

Another time on liberty I walked into my favorite café. It was my lucky day!

Three, not one, but three, cute young girls were sitting in a booth. I sat at the counter and pulled out some signalman cards. This was a few months before I became a yeoman/personnel man and transferred to ship's office. I was interested in becoming a signalman.

But there were "light signals" to learn for ships communication and also the "hand flags," etc. So many visual and alphabetical concepts were involved. The signalman flash cards were an excellent study guide.

The corner of my eye spotted one girl looking toward me maybe because I was a sailor, maybe inquisitive about the cards, maybe? Either way, it was the perfect opportunity to make a move. She was the beauty of the three: blond hair, blue eyes, a perfect Scandinavian. Without hesitation, I picked up the cards, walked over to the booth and sat down.

"I bet you wonder what I'm doing with these cards?"

That question started a friendship, a little romance with my girl from Kingsport, Tennessee, Billie Marie. She had won Miss Teenage Kingsport and I never did figure out if she had won Miss Teenage Tennessee, but she sure could have.

She was in San Diego with friends for the Church of God Youth Convention. We walked the streets of San Diego. We talked. We liked each other.

Billie Marie invited me to the last night of the convention. I don't remember much, except a large, large crowd.

Afterwards we went to her hotel room. Hundreds of people in one room! We found a darkened corner, our last night together. I stole a kiss. I stole a lot of kisses!

Many letters sailed through the fleet post office to the Tioga County. And many letters flew from the Tiger to Kingsport, Tennessee. I didn't need to find stamps while in Vietnamese waters, writing "free" in the upper right-hand corner served as a stamp.

Many months of corresponding soon grew tiring. Kingsport seemed a million miles away. And I think Billie Marie felt my ship was a million miles away. Letters between us became less frequent. The fire was dying. Without explanation we stopped writing. But I still had the "moments" with my Tennessee girl.

# Chapter 13
# Final Cruise

There were times in the Navy I thought survival was impossible. The loneliness and confinement sometimes made ship life unbearable. The faces were the same day after day. Other times being a sailor was fun, exciting, never dull. I loved sailing over the Pacific Ocean, the vast horizon, the Philippine Sea, jumping overboard for a swim, the South China Sea and even the Mekong Delta, at times.

As my tour of duty was approaching the end, with several months left, everyone in the ship's office wanted me to reenlist for four more years. I knew a Navy career was not exactly the life I wanted.

I didn't know at the time, but my final cruise would sail from Okinawa to Saigon; to Keelung, Formosa; to Japan and then to Pearl Harbor and San Diego.

Although there were sour memories at Naha, Okinawa, this time I was on my own ship. The Tiger was heavily loaded with tanks, trucks and jeeps. You could hardly walk on the main deck.

Going up the Saigon River, this time I managed to sneak topside, take some pictures and observe more than last time.

The huts along the river were built on high, heavy timbers, so flooding would not damage the dwelling. The huts were very close to the river. The Saigon River looked muddy, awfully muddy.

The Tioga beached at Saigon against a cement bulkhead. Everyone could see the city from the ship, but there was no liberty call. That hurt!

In the evening, a small wooden canoe was found near the ship with explosives. I was handed a rifle, a watch station near the end of the ship.

"If you see ANYTHING in the water shoot at it!"

After several days the ship was empty and headed back down the river. The next stop was Keelung, Formosa, for R and R.

"Request permission to leave the ship, Sir!" I saluted.

I checked to make sure I had my camera. I wanted to take many pictures of Keelung.

On the pier were several Pedi-cab drivers waiting to be hired. A Pedi-cab is basically a three-wheel bicycle with a large seat in the back.

One of the Chinamen waved at me and I waved back. It shouldn't cost too much in Formosa for a ride.

While I sat comfortably in the back seat, the driver asked in broken English several questions.

"Do you want to go drinking?"

"No."

"Do you want girls?"

"No."

"What do you want?"

"I want to see your city."

Off he pedaled with a smile on his face. Every once in a while, he'd ring his little bell and wave at Pedi-cab drivers with no passengers. He seemed proud to have an American sailor as a customer.

Soon my friend, for he was a friend, gave me some advice.

"If you want to buy something, let me buy it. People here will charge you too much."

Some beautiful watermelon caught my eye. I insisted he buy two big pieces. What a photo to treasure! My driver friend holding up two pieces of fresh Keelung watermelon! It was the best I ever tasted.

We came to a building and parked along the street. Climbing some stairs, I didn't know what to expect. Out of nowhere, several girls appeared at the top of the steps. Actually, I wouldn't call them girls. They were more like grandmas! I told the driver, "Thanks, but no thanks." And off we went.

What a way to see a city, riding and not walking. I was having a great time. But the greatest time was just ahead.

My driver friend asked if I wanted to meet his family. I would never pass up an opportunity to meet a Formosan family.

The Pedi-cab headed out of the city and soon we were surrounded by hills. We walked up a bank to a small hut. My driver invited me in and introduced his family, a large family, many sons and daughters.

100

The floor was di rt. There were windows, but no glass. Soon children were hanging in the windows trying to catch a glimpse of the "sailor." Children were everywhere.

My driver invited me to sit at a small table. He came with a small plate. On the plate was one clear egg. At first, I thought it was rotten. I didn't want to eat it! But the host was persistent and urged me to take a bite. Everyone was watching to see what I would do.

I took a bite. It was like rubber! The yoke was black. Later I learned it was a "special" egg and made me feel "special" also.

As we were leaving, it was time for picture taking.

Twelve of the children lined up outside the hut. I could not resist picking up the baby. When I kissed the baby on the forehead, the children laughed. The mother proudly held her baby up high for the camera. If I was running for a political office, I would have had everyone's vote.

Returning to the city, my Pedi-cab driver still had a smile on his face. And I did too!

One last stop before returning to the ship. My driver pulled up to a small outdoor counter. We sat down on stools and he ordered a drink. It looked clear, like bottled water. One sip proved the opposite. Strong! Strong! Strong!

I asked the driver what it was.

His laughing reply, "Rice wine."

It is impolite to let someone drink alone. I had to keep up with him.

By the time we reached the ship, all the rice wine had settled in my brain. I only remember the Pedi-cab driver refusing to take any money for the half-day ride. I did stuff some money into his pocket.

Next thing I remember I was sliding off the rack feeling a gigantic headache. After showering I hunted for my camera. I couldn't find it. It was lost!

Going topside to the main deck, I checked at the quartermaster's stand.

"Yes, a Pedi-cab driver came onboard last night and said a sailor left this camera in his backseat."

It was my camera. My camera with my pictures. He WAS my friend!

On the way to Japan, I helped prepare my new "orders." Two years of active duty were up. I was being discharged from the Navy. Soon I would be a civilian!

Of course, the first thing I noticed boarding the plane for San Diego were the stewardesses. Round eyes! Pretty uniforms. Pretty girls!

My assigned seat was in the very last row. Just before takeoff a stewardess asked if she could sit next to me. I didn't have to think that question over very long.

She was beautiful. She seemed genuinely interested in where my duty station was, what I did and where I had been.

As the conversation continued, I was thinking only one thought. "Thank you, God, for short skirts!"

# Chapter 14
# College Bound Again

Things would be different now. After two years of Navy life, many valuable lessons and experiences had changed me. The Navy did give an education I couldn't have received at a college or university.

Now, with the GI Bill I could return to college and start fresh in the academic field. It was the fall of 1967

I returned to Nampa, Idaho, for college. Only problem was, I did not anticipate the prolonged transition from military to civilian life. The evening news was constantly showing scenes from Vietnam. Newspapers had Vietnam as front-page stories. And college students were still marching, still burning and protesting. "The Vietnam Conflict" was still on!

It felt great being out of the Navy and back in school. I was meeting a lot of new and interesting students. But I had too much time on my hands, too many memories "stuck" in my head and too many fun things I wanted to do. Though I had enrolled, college was again drifting away, seeming less important each day. I hardly read a book or studied.

The following term I enrolled for only one class. I tried to convince myself I hadn't given up completely. It was at this time I started working for Albertson's grocery store. It was also when alcohol still had a tight grip on my life—a grip I was not aware of or simply one I did not want to confront.

Grocery stores in the late sixties did not have the modern scanners of today. The clerk had to work hard. Each item price had to be pressed by buttons on the cash register. For a $2.98 item, first you pressed the two button, then the period button, then the nine button, and finally the eight button. You pulled the levers down in different notches for the subtotal, to add taxes, then for the total, and finally pulled the levers down to open the cash register. Confusing? Yes, it was at first. Compared to scanners, the cash register was an antique.

People traffic in the store always brought enjoyment. From the little four-year-old blond, blue-eyed girl, to the big, blond, blue-eyed woman looking for love, no day was the same.

The little four-year-old, so cute with shiny blond hair and big blue eyes, came up and asked in deep earnest, "Hey, Mister, have you seen the Dough Boy?" Well, I had seen the Dough Boy on a television commercial.

"No, I haven't seen the Dough Boy. Let's see if we can find him."

First, we looked behind all the milk cartons, no Dough Boy. Then we checked the butter case, no Dough Boy. We looked and looked throughout the entire store, no Dough Boy.

No Dough Boy, but I had made a friend. Every time the little girl came into the store with her mom, she immediately found me to talk. She was my special little girlfriend.

The other big, blue-eyed blond was not looking for the Dough Boy; instead she was looking for love to forget a sad case of marital loneliness. I made her happy for one night, anyway.

Sometimes after work I'd go "cruising," as much as possible in a small Idaho town, with the guy working in the produce department. He drove a souped-up, slick, bright blue 1937 Ford pickup truck. It was a beautiful attention-getter, perfect for "Hey girls, want a ride?" The invitation was seldom refused.

This is how I met my Nampa girl, Valerie. She went from sitting on my lap in the pickup truck to an invitation for a swim at her house.

Her father owned a "mom and pop" grocery store; though not as wealthy as Joe Albertson, he could afford a covered swimming pool next to the house.

Just because she had recently graduated from high school, I was not going to let age interfere with a new romance.

Besides, there were no objections from her parents about the relationship. In fact, her mom was quite happy with the situation. Maybe because coming over after work, I always had a cold six-pack of beer. Like me, her mom loved beer!

Valerie had impressive qualities: style, class, warm-hearted, looked good in a bikini, but more important, liked to cuddle and kiss.

One winter evening we were sitting/lying on the sofa in the dimly lit living room around the fireplace. Yes, kissing and cuddling. Valerie's mom came into the room.

"Gene, you shouldn't be so close to the fireplace. You have ashes all over your face."

Ashes? No. Mascara? Yes.

I sensed Valerie's affection toward me was as strong as my devotion to her. She was the first girl I gave a small LP record to—B.J. Thomas's "Hooked on a Feeling."

The Navy taught many valuable lessons. One lesson I wish I hadn't learned was 'How to Become an Alcoholic.' Even though they sailed the seas a lot, sailors made up for the drinking on liberty. Actually, it was binge drinking every day until the ship sailed.

Being discharged from the Navy didn't discharge me from being an alcoholic. More and more of my time was spent in bars and taverns, playing pool and drinking.

It was a day off work, a day of fun. I was with a friend from the college called "Tuna" since he was so big. We started at three in the afternoon playing pool, drinking pitchers of beer, eating pizza and drinking pitcher after pitcher of beer.

"Hey, you ready to go?"

"Ya. Let's get out of here."

It was 11.30. I thought I'd better get out of the place before I was too intoxicated to walk. The pitchers of beer were beginning to look like glasses of beer.

Heading toward the college in my little white Volkswagen, we talked, laughed and joked about never, ever consuming so much beer in our lives!

Rounding a corner, I turned to talk to my friend…Instantly! Suddenly! CRASH! We hit something! Something very solid. The steering wheel was bent, the front window completely shattered. "Tuna" jumped out of the car, looked around. He couldn't see what I had hit. I just sat still. I was startled, scared, not hurt badly, just a sore wrist. My friend wasn't so lucky. As he got back in the car, blood dripped from several cuts on his forehead.

"Hey, you're hurt! We've got to get help!"

"No! I'm all right. Just get me back to the dorm!"

"But you're bleeding badly!"

"I'm OK. Let's get going!"

Before realizing the seriousness of the accident. I tried driving with the bent steering wheel toward the dorm. The little Volkswagen could run, but not fast. The front fender was dragging and the right door wouldn't close. After two miles we neared the college dorm.

"This is good. Stop."

My friend jumped out. I also got out, to check the front fender. It was smashed against the wheel. I pulled it away and headed back to my apartment.

What had I hit? A telephone pole? If I could just make it home and report the accident! I took the usual route from college. It brought me within a block of the accident scene.

Turning slowly around a corner, I pulled off toward the curb. The car was ready to quit, die. Looking around I saw red lights were flashing everywhere. A police car pulled in front of me, two more stopped in back. Oh no! Quick, don't let them know you've been drinking! I stepped out of the car.

"Could we please see your driver's license?"

The other two officers looked the car over.

"Have you been drinking?"

"Yes."

"What?"

Beer."

"How many glasses?"

"About eight." (More like eight pitchers plus.)

"What did you hit?"

"I think I hit a telephone pole."

The other two officers remarked, "There's red paint on the right front fender."

"And there's blood on the dashboard."

"I didn't have a passenger."

"Where did the blood come from?"

"Guess I had a bloody nose."

"Would you please step up to the sidewalk and walk a little ways?"

I walked down and then back, trying to be careful, trying not to appear drunk. It didn't work.

"OK, arrest him. On the way to the station, give him his rights."

Sitting in the small, southern Idaho jail, I felt sick—sick to my stomach from all the beer drinking. And mentally sick, wondering how I had ever ended up a place like this.

At five o'clock in the morning I was taken out of the cell, fingerprinted and had my picture taken. The officer seemed friendlier than the ones from the previous night.

"How do you feel?"

"Terrible!"

"Your passenger reported to the hospital last night."

"How is he?"

"He's going to be OK. Had about ten stitches put in his forehead."

"Oh no! What did we hit?"

"Another Volkswagen. No one was in it. The owner reported it stolen. You hit it into the next-door neighbor's porch. Lucky for you no one was in the other car. Oh, the dean of men from the college will be down to see you at about quarter to nine. You appear before the judge at nine."

As we headed back toward the cell, the officer stopped and directed me to a different cell.

"This one has a mattress on the bunk."

There were three other men in the cracker box cell: two elderly men, "shoplifting again," and a younger man wanted in another state.

When I stood before the judge, the dean of men from the college gave me at least a little support. The judge didn't want me to enter a plea until I had had time to consult an attorney. Bail was set at five hundred dollars. I remember thinking "FIVE HUNDRED DOLLARS! It might as well be five million. Where am I going to get that much money?"

The dean of men spoke up and asked the judge to release me into his custody. The judge agreed.

From jail I had to go immediately to work. At the store the newspaper had just arrived. On the front page, lower right-hand corner it read, "Student Arrested." After giving my name, address and details of the accident, it reported convicting charges.

"Drunk driving, leaving the scene of an accident, failure to render aid, failure to report an accident."

I explained the situation to the store manager. I was sick, tired, and needed another day off. He gave it to me.

In the evening one of the hardest things to do in my life was call home. I knew my parents would find out sooner or later. I wanted it to be sooner, by their son.

"Hello, Mom. You'd better get Dad. I want both of you to hear this I had an accident last night.

"Was anyone hurt?"

"Yes, but he's going to be OK. And there's something else…I was arrested for drunk driving."

"You WHAT?"

Then it came from both sides. I didn't say a word. There was nothing to say. I had known this would be the reaction. I knew they would say things from the "gut" and not the heart.

The next day at work, Mom called saying how sorry she was for everything said over the telephone. I felt better, but only for a short time.

The personnel committee at the college met with me and later agreed I could finish the term, but was ineligible to enroll the following term.

I don't think "sick" is a good descriptive word. Deep depression fits better. For a while I think I was just walking around in a daze, not really knowing or caring about anything—just wandering.

When the "crisis" settled down, Dad bought me a used government car at an auction. It didn't look like much, but was in great mechanical condition. He also loaned me more money for school, money I never had to repay.

There was some determination to make a success of college. Classes were becoming more interesting due to more serious studying, actually reading the assignments, turning in papers and passing exams.

College now had a bright side. Valerie, my little Nampa girl, had also enrolled in college. She wanted to pursue nursing. I still wasn't sure what I wanted.

When classes became difficult, comprehension weak, instead of "giving up," I searched out the professor. This solution proved successful most of the time.

A class on ethics was a prime example. The professor was a minister who had decided he wanted to teach. He had enrolled at Boston University, received a PhD, and graduated at the top of his class. He could have taught at any university in the United States or elsewhere. But instead he chose this little Christian college in a small southern Idaho town. He loved to teach.

One spring afternoon, the professor was lecturing, writing on the board, enthusiastically explaining a point when a riding lawnmower cruised past the window. The noise was very agitating to the professor, disrupting his thoughts.

When the mower came around a second time, he angrily threw his chalk at the opened window. The class softly chuckled, so did the professor.

Ethics class was getting touch. I knew I should seek help.

Walking into his office I didn't have much faith in myself or the professor's ability to stimulate the class. My attitude changed as we talked about his life and my life as a Vietnam Naval veteran. His compassion and empathy were acute. After giving me several study "tips," he showed me an excellent way to outline chapters in the ethics book.

For the final exam, I outlined all the chapters. Then I memorized the outline.

Standing at my table handing out the final exam bluebook scores, the professor paused with a huge smile. He handed me the bluebook.

B+! He didn't give A/s because he didn't think anyone was that smart in his class. For me it was an A!

Journalism and Creative Writing were two subjects that brought enjoyment and satisfaction.

The Nampa Free Press offered the journalism class an opportunity to help write and edit the newspaper for a day. The journalism professor, Miss Helen Wilson, chose me to be student editor. The newspaper ran an article explaining the upcoming venture. My picture was there. Thank God it was not a police mug shot!

Creative Writing class was not a class at all. On the first day the professor announced everyone should pick a topic or subject to write on for the term. There would be no class sessions—just weekly meetings, one-on-one, to show progress, complete professor evaluations, and solve any difficulties with the manuscript. The final grade was the final, completed manuscript.

I had a head start. Writing about Navy life, the Saigon River and Mekong Delta was already in a rough draft, after writing the experiences in my mind. The professor was very articulate, pointed out poor grammar, and made excellent comments/suggestions.

When I turned in the final manuscript I was satisfied. The A in Creative Writing was my only A in college. This is one class in which I wanted to excel.

One question written on the last page by the professor still rings in my mind, "Good writing! But what are you trying to say?"

World Literature introduced me to Zola's A PRIEST IN THE HOUSE and I found a small book in the college library by Leo Tolstoy. Not *War and Peace*, but "Childhood, boyhood, youth." Forty years later, with the help of Barnes & Noble, to my delight, I purchased "Childhood, boyhood, youth," to read again the creative and genius writing of Tolstoy.

I mention these two books because the writings were so unique and interesting. The impressions left were enduring.

As a private Christian college, NNC was able to foster and promote religious principles and ideals of the Church of the Nazarene. There were times of great spiritual renewal on the campus. It was almost as if God brought down a helicopter to spray love, causing renewed commitments to the student body. These were special times, sensing God's spirit, sensing God's love, sensing God was personal.

Wedding picture of sister and brother-in-law, Larry Hull, orthopedic surgeon

Mom's double wedding

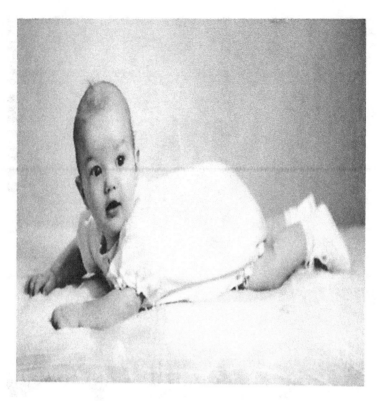

Wedding image, Seattle

i love you a bunch grandpa

Typical of the elementary school youngsters who make constant use of the Bothell Public Library are these from the Bothell Elementary school. Left to right are Gene Olson, fifth-grader; Corrine Knutsen, fifth-grader; Cheryl Bergren, sixth-grader; and Wayne DuBois, sixth-grader. Passage of a special two-mill levy to keep the library functioning is being sought of Town of Bothell voters in the Nov. 6 election.

(Citizen photo)

First time in newspaper

My mom and dad loved each other

I think my mom and dad looked like movie stars

I am 11 months older than my sister

First baby

George as a baby

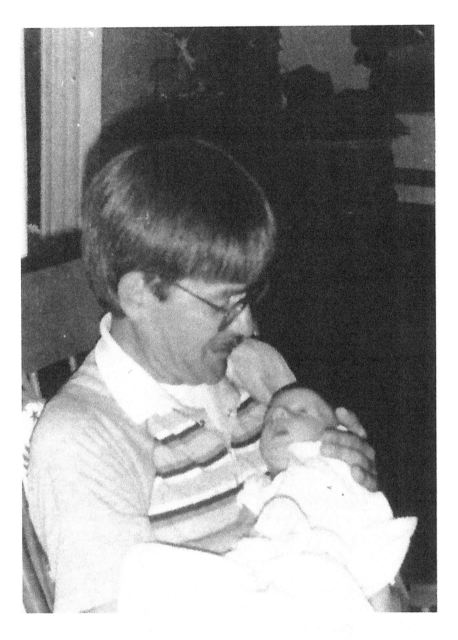

Gene-Paul as a baby

Living in Bellevue, WA

Sister giving me birthday cake

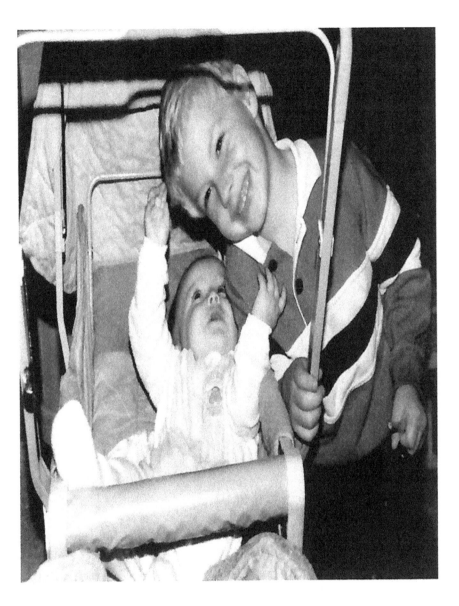

George and Gene-Paul playing

Grandpa loved Gene-Paul so, so much

Jolanta with cat at Centralia sister's house.

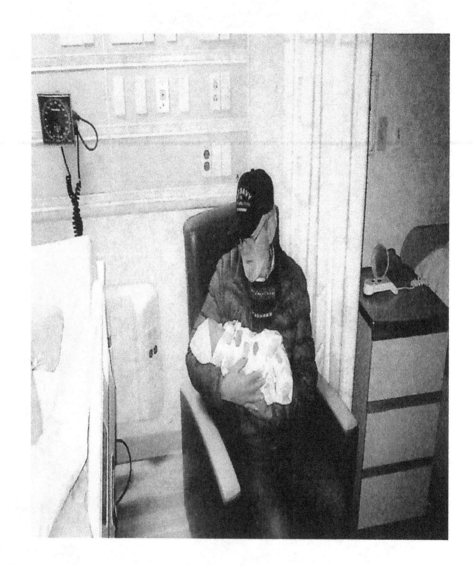

First grandson

Soldiers on ship

USS TIOGA COW NTY (EST 1158)

PN/YN Navy School

Ship anchored at Hong Kong

Seaman Olson (NAVY

Army on ship

Unloading trucks in Saigon

Tanks from Okinawa to Saigon

On a beach landing

Loading tanks for Saigon

Helicopter sometimes meant mail call

End of Typhoon

Veterans Day poster

Saigon River

Boot Camp Company 529

Senior High School photo

George and Gene-Paul at Pleasant Valley property

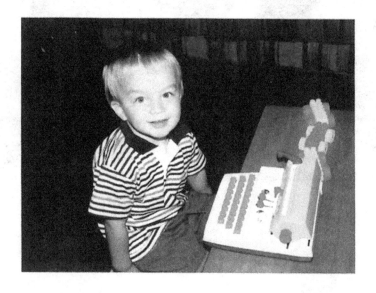

George wanted to type

At Mt. Saint Helens

Along Columbian River

The Olson Five

The Olson Five

With Gene-Paul at Indianapolis.

Gene-Paul cooling off

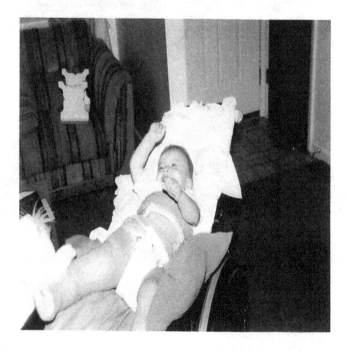

George had a dislocated hip surgery

Tired as a stay-at-home dad

Jolanta and Gene-Paul in Lynwood, WA

## Out of "Gene's" Pockets

By GENE OLSON

# What Are Intramurals

Intramural sports are organized programs of athletics. Intramurals were organized after a need was seen for branching away from interscholastic sports. Interscholastic sports were available only to the select few, being played between other schools. It was also noticed that more participation was needed regardless of playing ability. They saw the importance of everyone getting and keeping physically fit. As John F. Kennedy said in his Presidential Message to the schools on physical fitness of youth, "It is of great importance, then, that we take immediate steps to ensure that every American child be given the right to make and keep physically fit—fit to learn, fit to understand, to grow in grace and stature, to fully live."

"Youth Physical Fitness," a booklet published by the President's Council On Youth Fitness, states concerning intramural programs, "These programs should be conducted under competent leadership. The extended school day, noon hour, weekends, and the vacation periods should be replete with a variety of organized teams, leagues, tournaments, games, and special features. They should be skillfully planned and be as attractive and valuable to the pupil as interscholastic sports programs." Organized teams, leagues, tournaments, games, and special features all dealing with physical fitness are good examples of intramurals.

The question is then raised, who should sponsor a program of this type? Is it left entirely up to the school? Again the Cougar would like to quote President Kennedy: "In our total fitness efforts the schools, of course, will not stand alone. I urge that in all communities there be more coordination between the schools and the community, parents, educators and civic-minded citizens in carrying forward a resourceful, vigorous program for physical fitness—a program that will stir the imagination of our youth, calling on the toughest abilities, enlisting their greatest enthusiasm—a program which will enable them to build the energy and strength that is their American heritage."

## Off the Cuff

Hurrah! Hurrah! The new silver goal posts for our "practice" field have arrived. However, there still seems to be something missing from our new football field. Oh yes, those new lights and new stands. There is little hope left in the minds of this year's graduating class for a new football field. But, you sophomores and juniors, there is still hope for you. Leigh Mitchell Hodges once said, "Failure is often that early morning hour of darkness that precedes the dawning of the day of success." . . . Bob McGuire has the solution for getting rid of colds. The answer? Simple, instead of taking aspirin, just spread analgesic on your neck and tape it . . . What the paper staff would like to see is a Faculty-Varsity football game. Why not? They do it in basketball. Who do you think would win? . . . Speaking of intramurals we already have two football teams formed, Kenmore and Woodinville. First contest between the two teams ended Woodinville 84, Kenmore 48. But the Kenmore boys came back strong last week for a victorious battle 84-72. Don Martin, Woodinville had this to say about the game, "They cheated!" . . . What would the team do without Kirby Snyder? (Don't answer that) His humorous wittism keeps the team in stitches to and from away games. Keep up the good work Kirb . . . The following prayer is found in the football play book. Not only does it apply to Cougar athletes, but also to the sportsmanship of Cougar fans.

High school column in paper

UNITED STATES SENATE
WASHINGTON, D. C. 20510

JOHN KERRY
MASSACHUSETTS

September 21, 2011

Mr. Gene Olson
10708 NE 111th Court
Vancouver, WA 98662

Dear Gene,

Thank you for sending me your book *The Boy from Bothel*. I look forward to having the chance to read about your service in the Vietnam War and about your harrowing fight against bipolar disorder thereafter. As a fellow vet, I'm always interested to read about the stories of others from that time in our lives.

Your story will undoubtedly hit close to home for countless veterans still struggling – thanks again for sharing it and for thinking of me.

Sincerely,

John Kerry

*Take care and thank you!*

Letter from John Kerry

12 July 2011

Dear Mr. Olson,

Thank you for sending a personalized copy of your memoir, *The Boy from Bothell*. It is a very difficult task sharing such personal struggles, and I hope that the military experiences you relate and your battle with bipolar disorder will help others in similar circumstances.

Please accept my gratitude for your service to our Nation and your willingness to publish your story. My wife, Bonnie, and I wish you and your family all the best.

Semper Fidelis,

JAMES F. AMOS
General, U.S. Marine Corps
Commandant of the Marine Corps

Mr. Gene Olson
10708 NE 111th Court
Vancouver, WA 98662

# Vancouver vet revisits past in new book

**Gene Olson** started writing about his life as a means of therapy rather than from any desire to publish a book. As the chapters and stories began to build up, though, the 65-year-old Vancouver Navy veteran realized his tale could help others, he said.

So in early June he self-published his

**Gene Olson**

story, "The Boy from Bothell: Bipolar, Vietnam Veteran."

He hopes that by telling others about his mental "issues" — he hates the word "illness"— they won't feel as alone or frustrated, he said.

"I really think there is an answer," Olson said. "People shouldn't get discouraged if their medicine isn't working or people don't understand. There's always hope."

Olson, who takes lithium for the disease, said he dislikes calling it an illness because it sounds too final.

"If you have an issue you can get over it, if you have mental illness it sounds like you can't get over it — and that's not true," Olson said.

The book tells of how he moved from Navy service in Vietnam to college to the Seattle Veterans Administration psych ward and eventually to finding a medical solution and spiritual help through his Christian faith. The book will soon be available online at http://csnbooks.com/ and at http://amazon.com/, he said.

---

*Bits 'n' Pieces appears Mondays and Fridays. If you have a story you'd like to share, call Courtney Sherwood 360-735-4561, or e-mail features@columbian.com.*

# NNC Journalism Class To Assist With Edition

NAMPA — Northwest Nazarene College journalism students will put classroom knowledge into practice Saturday when they will help write and edit an edition of the Idaho Free Press.

Student editor for a day will be Gene Olson, freshman from Nampa.

Olson has named the following staff:

Linda Nichols, sophomore, Portland, managing editor; Eldon Book, junior, Nampa, sports editor; Gary Waller, freshman, Missoula, Mont., assistant sports editor; Doug Martin, freshman, Seattle, city editor; Jon Blinn, senior, Sparks, Nev., regional editor.

Kimberly Gray, freshman, Boise, and Ellen McDowell, freshman, Lisbon, N.D., wire editors; Nancy Anderson, freshman, Ridgefield, Wash., and Connie Bartz, freshman, Longmont, Colo., women's editors; April Tucker, freshman, Nampa, feature editor.

Reporters will be John Gibson, freshman, Portland, Tim Doramus, freshman, Middleton, Pam Boughton, freshman, Kent, Wash., and Darlene Eppes, freshman, Oak Harbor, Wash. Photographers will be Ray Ax, freshman, Nampa, and Art Abercrombie, senior, Anderson, Calif. Rewrite will be handled by Pat Kliewer, freshman, Wal-

GENE OLSON

nut Creek, Calif., and Hazel Allee, senior, Nampa.

This is the second year the Free Press has made available its facilities to the NNC journalism class.

Northwest Nazarene College, now Northwest Nazarene University

# Gene Olson

Gene Olson was born in Seattle, WA 1945 by a Swedish father and a Norwegian mother Bothell, WA is his hometown. He has traveled extensively in Europe, mostly Eastern Europe. He currently resides in Vancouver, WA. He loves the Columbia River. Every morning he can see Mt. St. Helens if it's not cloudy.

He drafted Army and released to the ... I served in Vietnam 1965-1967 in Amphibious Force onboard the LST ... City, making fetid trips along ... coast, cruising up Saigon River to ... and operations in Mekong Delta right in Dove loading up tanks ... a gap shipmate wanted me ... started an investigation with ONI of Naval Intelligence.

Here's how from Vietnam the ... diagnosed me as ... Schizophrenic. Six years later ... American Lake VA Medical ... Tacoma, WA, I was properly ... manic-depressive or new.

## Author Updates

## Books by Gene Olson

Showing 5 Results Books   Advanced Search

# City of Bothell™

Dear Mr. Olson,                    March 31, 2016

     Thank you so much for the books. They were a pleasant surprise. I had no idea that we had an author from Bothell.

Best Regards,

Darlene JK Duerr

Deputy Mayor, Bothell

Letter

# Suicide in Seattle

We sat together alone
Just two veterans
Alone on the 8$^{th}$ Floor
Waiting for the 7$^{th}$ Floor Psych Ward
Alone with messed up minds
He never spoke to me
I never spoke to him
We, sat in silence, staring
What was spinning in his head?
He just stared straight ahead
The wife came trying to communicate
But still staring, motionless
She left with a child unsuccessful

The morning came
Crying screams echoed at the hall
The wife was hysterical
Yelling, crying
Why did he do that?
Why did he remove the small window screen?
Why did he crawl eight floors to his death?
Was he hallucinating?
Did he want to die or just escape?
Question with no answer

The author of confusion won
The battle of good and evil continues.
Xylocaine. Xylocaine please stay away!

Nothing left, mouth pain
The Angels never came

The blood lady came with her basket
I'd give all the blood she wanted
Until my arm became blue, paralyzed
The Angels never came

Without warning
Lithium washed my mind
The angels never came
They were always there

(About my five months stay at American Lake VA Medical Center,
Tacoma WA)

She lit a cigarette
First her puff
Then mine
Angels can smoke

Finally outside with my Angel
Fresh air cold breeze
Squeezing hard on a rose stem
The thorns said, "You are alive!"

# The Blue Room

The blue room was blue
A dark blue light bulb
In the locked darkness
Shining bright blue

Spread eagle
Ankles leather strapped
Wrists leather strapped
Canvas tarp tied over body

I yelled, I screamed
Mouth no leather strap
Screamed at doctors
Screamed at politicians

Why locked Blue Room?
Pushed "Panic Button"
Fought with orderly
Punched his face on the floor

I woke in blue darkness
An angel was sitting next to me
Nurse Sarah
My comforting Angel

# The Angels Never Came

Strapped spread-eagled to my bed
I could not move beneath the tarp
Locked dark room—one blue light
The Angels never came

I yelled and screamed and cursed
President Nixon, VA Psychiatrists
Even yelled at God
The Angels never came

Free from straps
But still locked room
Blue light my only companion
The Angels never came

"I'll put you to sleep"
The dentist said
No, no, no!
The Angels never came

One by one all teeth came out

The Angels never came

Children I met during liberty

My first car, a 1955 Chevy Hardtop

# The Cross from the Boys Home

When my father retired from the boys' home there was a box in the alcove with various items in it. On the top was a cross that Dad had on this wall. The arm was broken and itwas a faded gray. I put some superglue on the arm and then took Jesus off the cross. I painted him a clear white and also put red paint for his wombs. Then I placed Jesus onmy wall in my office. Every day I can see Jesus.

# Chapter 15
# Seeds of Manic Depression Germinate

The treasure valley of Idaho—Boise, Nampa, Caldwell—had become my home. The hot summers and snowy winters, compared to the Pacific Northwest rains, appealed to me. Perhaps the weather in Southeast Asia bears responsibility.

There was also the joy of independence. I was on my own, free, able to drink and smoke if that was my desire, and do things without worrying about "sinning here and sinning there." No one was my judge.

After two years with my sweet Nampa girl, the relationship had slowly cooled, slowly faded, slowly ended—something that had happened before.

Back in Washington State, my parents started two group homes for boys. One in Bothell, Washington, was called Evergreen Heights Boys' Home. The homes were named "Evergreen" since Washington was the Evergreen State.

It was always a problem to find good, dedicated people to fill staff positions. Low salary and the difficulty of being a childcare worker compounded the situation. So, my parents had a "great idea." They asked me to work at the boys' homes for the summer.

After some contemplation, I agreed to return to Washington State and work in the boys' homes. I never returned to southern Idaho. I never returned to the Treasure Valley.

It was tough working for family. Mother directed the boys' home in Arlington. Father directed the boys' home in Bothell. I floated between both. My older brother George was the social worker, having a master's degree in social work from the University of Washington.

All boys were wards of the state of Washington. There were about fifteen boys in each home. Thirty tangled-up lives of mere nine-to-twelve-year-olds with no understanding, no hope, no future.

What was "THE EVERGREEN BOY?" An excerpt from a staff "orientation" page described:

THE EVERGREEN BOY

He's a boy yet he's different because of his experiences. He doesn't know how to relate and communicate.

1. Verbally he communicates through explosive outbursts. He usually has never experienced a "chat."
2. He'll withdraw and use silence. He's either angry or lost for words.
3. He'll hit someone (a peer) or something. Again, he doesn't know how to say it, he has to act it.

LISTEN YES, BUT NOT SO MUCH TO THE WORDS AS TO THE FEELINGS AND ACTIONS.

He expects punishment but he usually expects physical or humiliating actions. It is what he's used to and expects!

Surprise him, don't react like he expects. He won't believe you at first. He'll think you are trying to con him so he'll test to prove to himself you are just like the others. After several tries, he'll start to get the message, then we've started to help him.

He comes knowing one thing – LOOK OUT FOR YOURSELF. NOBODY CARES FOR ME. Show him he's wrong and that he has to be a part and still a person...

Yes, it was rough working for family, but extremely difficult dealing with young, incorrigible boys. I was bewildered to see such sadness and confusion in a small body.

One boy had been sexually abused by his father. He never wanted to discuss it for a long time. When he did start to talk, nothing was left out. In graphic detail, he spoke and spoke about what his father had done to him and his body.

Another boy had been locked in a closet several days for having a bad temper, etc.

One boy's father ran off with a seventeen-year-old babysitter, then tried to kill his mother by running her down with a car. The boy was in the car.

The list goes on from arson to LSD, to drug abuse.

The group home structure tried to give an alternative to dysfunctional family situations, more stability, better feelings of self-worth and positive future planning.

Time away from the boys was cherished and needed. It was hard to separate the emotions you felt for the boys and the task of modifying their behaviors, attitudes and feelings. Sometimes there were results, steps forward. Other times no results, steps backwards.

Days off were special. It was good to be completely away from the boys and the home in general. If it was sunny, I'd head for one of my favorite beaches on Lake Washington, Juanita Beach, where I had learned to face-float in grade school, and Waverly Beach, closer to Kirkland, but much smaller.

I could swim, lie in the sun, close my eyes and be at China Beach, South Vietnam, or any place I had traveled. The great thing was when I opened my eyes I was still in the United States.

It was also on the beach I worked on the "project" "Jesus Christ Superstar." I had a cassette recorder, "Jesus Christ Superstar" cassette tape and music score. Around five hundred color slides, mostly of Southeast Asia and the Navy, were in my mind on a memory disc. As the music for "Jesus Christ Superstar" played, I thought about the best color slide for that moment. I had enough images! The problem was arranging them in proper order.

People passing by with curiosity just had to ask questions. "Is the musical 'Jesus Christ Superstar' coming to Seattle?"

"Are you going to be in it?"

I played the cassette tape over and over and over, again and again. I needed to get the feel, mood and ideas for present and future pictures.

On my trips back and forth to Juanita Beach, it became apparent there was a drug problem at the beach. Several kids would gather on a lawn left of the beach entrance. You didn't have to be too intelligent to observe and understand what was taking place.

A boating accident near the swimming area pushed me even deeper into the problem.

Sunning after a swim on the beach, I noticed a commotion disrupting the peace. A lifeguard was running from the first aid station, running fast. The first thought to come was maybe this was a rare opportunity for unique pictures. Grabbing the camera, I followed the lifeguard.

A small ski boat was drifting toward the shore. Wading into the water, I waited for the boat to beach. Soon a large crowd emerged to observe the incident.

The lifeguard worked feverishly to stop the bleeding of an injured swimmer, applying bandages and shouting out orders. The crowd was silent, stunned. We all were swimmers!

The fire department's first aid wagon rushed to the scene. As the swimmer was lifted out of the speed boat, the whiteness of his body showed evidence of shock.

It was traumatic for me. He had been run over with spinning sharp propellers, spinning fast! As a water-skier, I dreaded thinking about falling in the water and a speeding boat not paying attention and slicing over me like this skier. Or, to be driving a speed boat, suddenly see a skier ahead and not be able to stop soon enough. Then it was too late!

Since I already had photographs, I thought it might be a good idea to write a freelance article on "Waterskiing Safety" or something. I was still writing, mostly in my mind and mostly receiving "rejection slips."

Shortly the King County Shore Patrol boat arrived for an investigation. Approaching their boat, I was still thinking about the article and how I could use an interview with the two officers.

After talking for a while I presented my ideas and asked if they would consent to a taped interview. The idea didn't appeal to them.

"We aren't authorized to do that sort of thing without permission."

When I mentioned pictures of the accident, well, pictures taken at the end of the lifeguard carrying him out of the boat, etc., the King County Shore Patrol asked for the film.

If they weren't going to help me, I wasn't going to help them. I knew my rights. No, you can't have my film."

The look on the officers' faces was one of contempt. They did ask for my name, address and phone number. That I would give.

While questioning several people on the beach, I found it wasn't long before I had several names and telephone numbers. Most of the kids that hung out at the corner entrance were friends of the injured skier.

The driver of the boat was the hardest to collect any information about. The only thing I could find out was he came from a wealthy family. His father owned several large apartment buildings on the east side of Lake Washington.

I arranged to have a meeting with him one night, but no one showed up. I wanted to interview both sides.

Rumors drifted around the beach that the driver of the bot was in jail. He had been under the influence of either alcohol or drugs while driving the boat. Rumor also said a possible lawsuit might develop.

After visiting the injured water skier in the hospital, I knew he was very lucky. With only a punctured lung and several broken ribs, he would soon be back 100 percent.

I wanted to find out how the police could use my pictures. The easiest thing was to just go to the nearest town's police department, in Kirkland. I asked several kids at the beach who was a good policeman to chat with. A sergeant's name was frequently given, so I figured he was the man.

The sergeant was very cordial and I could see and sense why he was well-liked, respected and popular. He invited me to his office and we talked for a long time.

He said in a court case, just any pictures near the scene of the accident could be useful. I mentioned my concern with the drug problems at Juanita Beach. He disclosed a problem in the park on a hill in back overlooking the police station. Something was going on up there, but they just didn't know what it was.

Leaving the police station, I decided to take a look at the hill park. When I arrived, it was dark, the park appeared empty. I sat down on the lawn and played "Jesus Christ Superstar" on the cassette. Looking, observing, I noticed a small gully in the grassy hill. A person could lie down without being seen and have a complete view of the police station.

I sensed I was being observed, but it was too dark to notice anything. Getting up to leave, I quickly turned around and noticed several young boys creeping down, as if they were following me.

"What do you guys want?" I asked.

They came closer, talked small talk for a while and then returned to the gully. As I was getting into the car to leave, I heard a chant coming from the boys.

"NARC! NARC! NARC! NARC!"

The next day I revisited the police department and decided to investigate the park area while it was light.

Reaching the area from the night before, I stopped abruptly. My attention was quickly diverted to a bright orange spray-painted message, "F…you, Pig!"

It didn't stop me from going to Kirkland or Juanita Beach. The beaches were a great retreat from the boys' homes.

But one evening was the start of my first manic high.

I was in Kirkland, driving the old gray government Ford near the hill behind the police station. A car started following very closely, too closely. I sped up. The car sped up. I felt the person was trying to "drive" me out of Kirkland.

Once I was out of the city limits, the car disappeared. I wasn't sure what to think.

It was night. I kept driving on Juanita Drive along Lake Washington. My mind was concentrating on kids, drugs, skiing accidents and what was happening around me.

I kept driving. My imagination and creativity took control. I drove over the bridge by the boat ramp where the Sammamish River flowed into Lake Washington. Nearby was the Kenmore Air Harbor. I thought it would be a perfect place to smuggle drugs. Have a boat ready for Seattle and cruise up the river to Lake Sammamish. The seaplane had a perfect disguise, charter flights.

Within minutes, I spotted a sheriff's car coming out of a darkened driveway. It could be a stakeout.

By now it was early morning. I kept driving and driving. I always went the same route. Over and over again. It was almost like being hypnotized, as if I had no control.

I would drive as far as my favorite pancake house in Lynnwood; turn around and head back to Juanita Drive to Kirkland. Same route, same fifteen-plus miles each way.

Driving down the hill on Juanita Drive close to the Ingelmoore Country Club I slowed down. There was something sitting on the bank hiding in the thick bushes.

There were no other cars in sight on the road. I stopped, backed up.

Sitting so still was a beautiful German shepherd dog. It could have been a stuffed dog.

I whistled at it. No movement. I tried everything to get the dog to move. It didn't budge an inch.

Why was it there? Police dog! This was a police dog. Was a drug shipment coming through? This was the night. Something was going to happen. And I was going to be there. My manic mind started rolling again.

Several miles down the road a Washington state patrolman stopped a car. He was checking I.D. and the car's registration. An hour later another car had been pulled over—a lot of activity for a small two-lane highway at this time of night.

I continued driving. Nothing else was happening, but I kept driving over and over the same route. Over and over again.

Turning around in a parking lot close to the pancake house, I paused. Two Lynnwood policemen were standing, talking, by their patrol cars. I didn't know why they were there, but perhaps I needed a break and to go to the pancake house.

As I walked in, there was a man in a center booth; off to the left were the cook and a man dressed in an old, dirty Snohomish County sheriff's uniform. He didn't look like a sheriff. At another table there were four men.

The man in the center booth was watching me closely and also glancing around, especially looking out the window. He looked suspicious and nervous. Being in a high condition, almost losing touch with reality, I decided to strike up a conversation. "Hi. My name is Gene Olson, what's yours?"

That really made him nervous. He didn't answer, just wiggled around and glanced out the window again.

I decided to leave.

Walking to my car in the parking lot, I reached for my keys. Looking up I noticed four men heading toward me. Around the corner, a car, an old sheriff's car, slowly pulled around the parking lot toward us. The men stood around me in a circle, like they were shielding me from the car. Hey, what's going here?" I asked.

"You don't know?" came a reply.

"No," I answered.

They never told me.

As the car drove by, the men left keeping their eyes on the driver at all times.

In the car, I was not tired. But it was time to drive home. Too many thoughts, ideas, spinning too fast.

Off Bothell Way, I decided to take a shortcut up Pontius Road to home.

What happened three miles up the road is a mystery. I woke up by the side of the road with an empty tank of gas. Cars were speeding past, so it seemed.

I walked to a nearby house and called the gas station where my dad had an account. They would bring some gas "as soon as possible." The "soon" turned out to be an hour later.

Within that time a car stopped next to mine. Two men, in suits, an old car and a question.

"Why don't you go to Mukilteo?" one asked.

Mukilteo? Thoughts flashed. I was confused. The only thing at Mukilteo was the ferry to Whidbey Island. And Whidbey Island is home for the Naval Air Station.

The men drove off, asking only that one question.

Gas finally arrived.

Back at the gas station there were two "Hell's-Angels"-type motorcyclists at the gas pump. One guy was sitting on his bike with the gas hose in the tank, fumbling with a lighter, trying to light a cigarette, putting on a show.

While getting gas, I left the trunk opened to return the gas can and went into the office to sign. From the window I saw a neatly dressed, suited man investigating my trunk, going through my backpack and searching everything there.

Being tired and confused, it didn't bother me. I didn't care; I didn't even ask what he was doing.

My car full of gas, I was too exhausted to explore Mukilteo. I was only a mile from home. That sounded good!

Dad was driving down the road.

"Where have you been? We've been worried about you all night." "I don't want to talk about it, Dad. I went to my room and cried.

# Chapter 16
# Return to the Pancake House

The pancake house was still a favorite stopping place, despite recent unexplainable and mysterious events. It was easy access off the 1–5 Freeway for the thirty-mile drive to Arlington and Evergreen Park Home.

Six o'clock in the morning, I needed coffee, not so much pancakes, but a good pitcher of coffee. I liked the idea of a pitcher; you never had to keep asking the waitress for a refill.

Opening the door, I noticed two neatly dressed men in suits (I was seeing a lot of "neatly dressed" men lately) following me in, either by chance or plan.

They sat in a booth adjacent to mine. I was drinking coffee and reading an old paperback book. One of the gentlemen started a conversation.

"What are you reading?"

"*Man's Search for Meaning*."

Both men observed me closely.

The conversation continued with them asking my name and other personal questions. At first, I thought they were life insurance salesmen. But then a question out of nowhere aroused my curiosity.

"We want to know your views on money . . ."I replied with the first thought that entered my mind, "If you laid one hundred dollars down on the table, I wouldn't take it." Why had I said that?

They continued talking—this time about Bangladesh and money.

"We're not talking about a few hundred dollars, but large amounts of money. We have a color slide presentation we think you'd be interested in. Would you rather see it in Marysville or Bellevue?"

"Bellevue."

It was closer to home and on the east side. The east side They wrote down a name and phone number to contact.

But something just didn't seem right. Both men acted as if they were hiding something. I couldn't explain it. I couldn't make any sense of it.

As we were leaving one man asked, "Do you like children?" Naturally I answered, "Yes."

"So, do I. I have three of my own."

They wouldn't give me their own phone numbers. Instead, the other man said, "Give him this number."

All day at work I thought about the morning conversation. The more I thought about it, the more suspicious I became. Something wasn't right. I sensed some type of trouble, but what? I wasn't sure about the east side.

I didn't want anything to do with these two men. I tore up the piece of paper and flushed it down the toilet.

At the time I thought I was making the right decision. Now I don't know. I'm still curious. Maybe I should have called the number. Maybe I'll never know the truth. Bipolar seeds were starting to sprout. Paranoia was growing at a rapid pace.

# Chapter 17
# Vietnam and Rich

Rich was on my mind constantly. Since returning from Idaho, I hadn't talked with his dad at the bank. I was a veteran now and wanted to know what was going on with Rich's life. Was he still a helicopter pilot? Was he out of the army?

The bank lobby was the same. Rich's dad was standing tall, but gone was his usual familiar broad smile and hand wave. I asked the question I had always asked.

"How's Rich?"

His eyes swelled, holding back tears within so as not to cry. And with a crackled voice he told me his sorrow.

"Rich was killed in Vietnam. His helicopter was shot down. They never found his body."

Killed in Vietnam!

I left the bank, but I don't remember. I don't remember where I went. I didn't remember anything for several days.

The family sensed strange and unusual behaviors in my personality. This was probably why I was invited to spend the night at my sister's and brother-in-law's house—perhaps for an assessment of the situation.

Morning breakfast brought a comment from my sister. "There is a problem." There was a problem, but why?

I left her house driving down 45th toward the university district. At the middle of the bridge over 1–5, a Seattle police car was slowly coming down the off ramp. The ramp to the freeway was to the left, the one I wanted. Another Seattle police car was slowly moving into the freeway. Something was going on. But what?

Rich was still on my mind as I drove north on the freeway toward Bothell. There was a tape in my brain, manic moments from the second grade, junior high and high school. The problem was I had no stop button! It just kept playing.

I wanted to find out more about Rich and what had happened in Vietnam. The Bothell police station might have some answers.

The policewoman at the desk appeared sloppily dressed; her uniform needed ironing. She was nervous and just seemed out of place. Before I had a chance to open my mouth, she asked, "What is it, Gene? What's the matter?"

I felt trapped! I didn't know what was going on. How had she known my name? I hadn't given it. Why did she think something was wrong?

She left the front desk, went back and pressed a button that "clicked" like a tape recorder.

That did it! I turned and raced out the door never saying a word.

I wanted to talk with Rich's dad again. Just before the sharp curve on Bothell Way coming into Bothell, with the sigh "Welcome to Bothell. Stay for a day or a lifetime," high on top of Norway Hill, was Rich's house. I headed there.

All the yeas living in Bothell I had never visited Norway Hill. I didn't know where I was driving. I didn't get lost.

When I reached the top Rich's, dad was standing in the driveway as if he had known I was coming. Perhaps the Bothell police called saying, "Look out, Mr. Worthington, Gene is on his way."

The view was spectacular with the sun setting in the west; I thought I could see faraway Puget Sound.

We talked, but I don't remember for how long or what about, until the conversation turned to Rich's mom.

Rich's mom hasn't been feeling very well lately. She's sick in bed. I bet she would really like to see you. Would you like to come into the house and see her?" Of course, I would, and I did.

I had to tell her how much fun I had had at Rich's second grade birthday party. The little red twin-engine airplane I had received still flew in my mind. And I had to talk about the junior high incident when Rich and I were horsing around. He had knocked me out unintentionally. The teacher had wanted to put a Band-Aid on the cut above my eye. But Rich had said, "You don't need a Band-Aid, Gene; God will heal it." I didn't know if Rich had told his mom the story.

That was the last time I saw Rich's dad and mom.

But I still see and hear Rich's dad in the bank lobby. I still see a broken heart. I still hear sadness and grief.

# Chapter 18
# Fairfax Psychiatric Hospital

"I want you to come with me to see a psychiatrist."

It did not surprise me to hear Dad's voice of concern. The all-night drive was a mystery to him and to me. He had seen changes taking place. Reluctant at first, now he knew something was wrong; professional advice was needed. But Dad didn't know about Rich, the helicopter crash, his death in Vietnam and the details of the all-night drive.

When he asked me if I would go with him to see a psychiatrist, I went only to make him feel more at ease. As far as I was concerned, I didn't need professional help.

The doctor's clinic was in downtown Seattle just south of the Westin Hotel near the Seattle center monorail tracks. He was recommended by my brother-in-law the doctor as a very qualified Christian psychiatrist. I guess a "Christian" psychiatrist attends church on Sundays and a "non-Christian" psychiatrist goes skiing in the mountains on Sundays. I didn't care what the psychiatrist was either way.

The consultation was quick. After asking several short questions of me, he turned to Dad.

"I think he should be hospitalized."

Hospitalized! Was I that bad off?

"I'd like him to go to Fairfax Psychiatric Hospital." I'd never heard of Fairfax, so I asked where it was.

"It's in Kirkland, on the east side of Lake Washington."

"No!" I screamed, placing my head in my hands.

Kirkland was the last place I wanted to be. Kirkland had started all this crap!

No one knew the reasoning behind my scream. No one knew the spinning, twirling thoughts racing, racing faster and faster. No one could find the off switch; neither could l. Here I was twenty-six years old, ready for the journey from paranoid schizophrenic to manic depressive/bipolar.

My dad and I arrived in Fairfax in the late afternoon. It was less than a mile from Juanita Beach, but appeared to be a nice, fairly new hospital. We went into a small room and waited for the doctor.

The doctor walked into the room with a syringe.

"No, I don't want a shot!"

Who knows what could have been in the syringe? Poison! I could be killed! I was persistent. The doctor left.

When he returned, I was startled. Something was wrong. It wasn't the same doctor, or so I felt. His hair was different. This time, I was to swallow a pill. I didn't like that idea either, but after some persuasion agreed to it.

Dad left and I started to explore the hospital and hallways. I walked into a room eventually to be familiar on all psych wards, the day room. Two men were sitting on a sofa with nice-looking suits. Here we went again with men in suits! As soon as they saw me, they got up and left. Not very friendly. . .

Over by the television a teenage girl was kneeling close up. She slipped her breast from her bra and pressed it against the face of the TV weatherman. I was in no condition to be sexually aroused by a breast squished against a TV screen, but I figured this was the right place for her.

As I was walking down the hallway, a man slowly passed by and whispered, "There are cameras in here." Great! As if I wasn't paranoid enough. Now where were the cameras?

One bulletin board caught my attention. There was a gray, cloth-stuffed animal tacked on a corkboard. As I touched it with my fingers, it became very warm. I thought maybe there was an explosive device inside.

At the bottom of the bulletin board was a three-by-five card with a typed message, "Patients who are deeply disturbed should go to the front lobby." I was deeply disturbed.

I had an idea. Not only would I go to the front lobby but everything on the bulletin board would also go to the front lobby. All the artwork, lettering, cloth animals, and tacks were deposited piece by piece to the front lobby. It took a while, but I was successful.

It wasn't long before several nurses had me cornered, along with two big orderlies. I was escorted to the front of the closed ward. Waiting for me was a wheelchair and gurney. I knew they were going to give me a shot, but I fought hard the best I could. I was outnumbered.

After the injection I was tied to the wheelchair.

I awoke with a "snap!" sound from a stick match burning, in the darkness, in front of my eyes, as I was still strapped to the gurney. This was my introduction to Mario, a patient from the Walla Walla State Prison in Washington.

I was in the locked ward, but I had no mobility on the ward since my room was also locked.

Mealtimes were preceded by the sounds of a key in the door and an arm stretching around blindly, laying a tray on a nightstand by the door. Was that a man's or a woman's arm? What were they so afraid of?

The first session with my psychiatrist was something I looked forward to. I had asked for a large piece of construction paper, several newspapers, and magazines. I made a collage for the doctor. Since I had no scissors, I tore out phrases, headlines and pictures to convey how I was feeling, what thoughts were twirling.

One picture in particular was from the Seattle Post-Intelligencer. There was going to be a marksmanship competition in Seattle. The picture accompanying the article was a large handgun facing the reader.

There was no glue, everything was lying loose.

Still in a locked room, I presented the collage to my doctor. He stared at it for several minutes. I waited anxiously. It was a good collage.

"You are sicker than I thought."

What? Sicker? Take another look!

That's it, all I recall about our first session. I didn't know then it would be our last.

Brother George was the next visitor. He asked before he came if I wanted anything.

"Some Camel filter cigarettes."

I heard the key. George came in with a carton of Camel filters and stood at the end of the bed. The expression on his face was one of sadness and disgust. I'd never seen this look from my brother before. What was he looking at?

As someone who didn't smoke, I thanked him for the carton. I had been expecting just a pack.

Graduation came from the locked room to the locked ward.

The first assignment was a shower. It turned into a disaster. An orderly escorted me to this little tiny room. Once I was inside, the door shut and locked automatically. I couldn't open the door! I panicked! I pounded, screamed, knocked hard; someone came and opened the door. The lock was explained.

Having the room unlocked gave me more freedom to move and walk throughout the closed ward...well, some freedom of movement.

Mario reappeared. I would find out not only was he a convict but he had a severe brain tumor.

He never spoke a word. He talked with facial expressions and arm and hand movements. Perhaps a language learned in prison or the result of brain damage.

Mario was my protector. If I didn't respond to his gestures, go or do what he wanted anger filled his face.

Once a very old patient passed me in the hallway with his wife. He opened his robe and exposed himself to me. I didn't think men that old could get an erection. But it reinforced the fact of "dirty old men."

Out of frustration and no place to go, I spent a lot of time walking the hallway of the L-shaped locked ward.

This is when I met Josephine. I wasn't sure if Josephine was a man or a woman. She looked crazy. I'm sure I did too.

I was the only one "walking" the closed ward, until Josephine decided to join in. She started following me, but I kept a good distance away. If I stopped, she seemed frightened and went the other way. I was frightened also.

She kept reaching down as if to fix her socks or get something from her socks.

I took a detour into the TV lounge, a place I never went. A cooking show was on.

The chef appeared very nervous as he was chopping food.

He kept saying, "She's got a knife. She's got a knife."

I was reminded of cameras. Several years ago I had read a newspaper article about people watching TV in the future and their room could be observed by others—a two-way camera setup.

Josephine and I continued our cat-and-mouse game in the ward's hallway. I was getting tired and saw the ridiculousness of the fear and unknown. I stopped. That's it! How many hours?

I was afraid. I stretched out my arm and hand in back. I looked away straight forward, not wanting to see.

Josephine touched the tips of my fingers. She just wanted to touch me!

Minutes later the side doors to a grassy fenced patio were unlocked and two chaise lounges carried out, one for Josephine and one for me.

We lounged for a while in the warm sun, faces cooled by a light breeze. For the first time in a long time, there was an outside world. No one ever spoke.

Then Josephine asked a question.

"Are you Gene Olson?"

"Yes."

No other words were spoken.

In the evening Josephine's family came to visit. It was dark. A side door was unlocked. A bright spotlight was shining on a group of people, arranged like a family portrait. Josephine was sitting in the middle of the front row. There were about four rows. Everyone was dressed in black and wore derby-type hats. Not one person moved as if waiting for the camera to flash.

I was afraid to approach them because I didn't know what was happening. If it was a hallucination, it was the best one I'd ever had!

The next day Josephine was gone.

In a few days I moved out of the locked ward. More freedom, more places to explore.

Playing pool occupied most of my time. Once several young visitors played in the pool room.

Like Josephine, one teenager asked only one question.

"Are you Gene Olson?"

"Yes, I am."

Without saying a word, everyone placed their cue sticks on the table and quickly left.

Another weird piece of a strange puzzle.

Private psychiatric hospitals are expensive. After about five weeks money was becoming scarce. My brother found out I was eligible for psychiatric treatment at the VA Medical Center in Seattle. Treatment at the time was free regardless of personal income. As a Vietnam veteran I had priority over other veterans except those with service-connected disabilities.

Riding with the top down in my brother's little blue Fiat, seeing the floating bridge with Seattle ahead, made me happy for freedom once more. Fairfax, Kirkland was behind. I didn't look back. I wanted to forget the hospital. I wanted to forget the time spent. But I never would.

# Chapter 19
# Seattle Veterans Administration Medical Center

The VA hospital sits high on Beacon Hill overlooking a panoramic view of downtown Seattle. I found myself on the eighth floor, too high, but if I didn't look out the windows, I was OK.

Dr. Hague, a big man, a cordial man, was my first VA doctor. He had a corncob pipe that brought him much enjoyment; he was always lighting it, slowly inhaling the hot tobacco and exhaling as he asked questions. He paused between questions in deep thought. I liked him. I thought it was too bad he couldn't afford a nicer pipe,

Lastly, he performed a physical examination, an exam Fairfax Hospital had never done.

There were only two of us veterans in the day room, probably the only ones on the entire eighth floor. I didn't know the other patient's name, where he was from, nothing. He sat motionless, staring straight ahead in silence. I wondered what was going through his mind. Maybe he felt the same toward me.

His wife would come visit with a little girl. She would speak as if a conversation was going on. But there was none, only her lone voice with no response. She still talked as though hoping to break the silence. It was never broken. She would leave unsuccessful. He was still, silent, like when she came.

The morning in the day room was interrupted by cries, screams, wailing from the outer hallway. During the night the veteran had committed suicide; her husband was dead.

He had pulled a small screen off the window, wiggled through—which to me seemed impossible—and had fallen eight stories below onto a sidewalk. A nurse coming to work had discovered the body, dead.

As a child I had wanted to know what "suicide" meant. The answer was difficult to understand. Why would someone want to die, to kill themselves? I had asked God to explain it. He hadn't.

I wondered if this veteran had truly wanted to die. Maybe he was hallucinating wanted to leave, and thought the window was a door? Maybe his mind became so confused, tormented; he had to escape the room, the hospital, at any cost?

I asked God to explain it. He didn't.

The seventh floor was the locked ward. I moved in as a paranoid schizophrenic, an easy label covering a wide path in the mental health field. In the early seventies, I think every person with mental problems was diagnosed as "paranoid schizophrenic." Seems to me the labels should read "Paranoid Schizophrenic Type A," "Paranoid Schizophrenic Type B," "Paranoid Schizophrenic Type C," and go through the entire alphabet, then start all over: Type A-I Type B-l. Type C-1," etc. That would be good!

More than six million American adults suffer from bipolar disorder (manic depression) and/or schizophrenia. These are two of the most severe and crippling forms of mental illness.

What medicine do you give a paranoid schizophrenic? The old standby, Thorazine. Thorazine has helped clear out many state hospitals. Between 1965 and 1980, state hospital mental patients went from 470,000 to a staggering 100,000.

What medicine do you give a paranoid schizophrenic on a VA psych ward? Liquid Thorazine. Liquid Thorazine in the morning. Liquid Thorazine in the afternoon. Liquid Thorazine in the evening. Pump in as much liquid Thorazine as possible. Some people call liquid Thorazine a chemical lobotomy, some call it a chemical straightjacket, but I call it "the devil's brew."

I think the drug should be called "liquid zombie." I don't mean a cocktail containing rum, fruit juices and soda. After drinking liquid Thorazine, you develop "zombie" characteristics of "slow motion," "walking on eggs, stiff arms," "dry mouth," and "loss of long-term memory." I never wanted to sleep very much; I was just in a continual dazed state. It did slow down the twirling, rapid thoughts and ideas that had controlled me before. But it was a sudden contrast being a "zombie.' Perhaps it was what I needed at the time.

Those conditions were not unusual, since most veterans on the closed ward acted the same way.

Some patients remain more vivid than others—the tall, elderly "Texas" cowboy, with a big cowboy hat, cowboy shirt, cowboy boots, continually grinding, grinding his teeth. It was almost enough to drive you crazy.

The Jewish kid who wondered, like us all, what were we doing here? His mother visited every night.

Another veteran had electric shock treatments. I watched as the staff and doctors hooked up the wires to his head, then had to leave. His front silver-capped tooth shot out someplace. Shock treatments for depression—sometimes it worked. Veteran Willie had a beautiful four-year-old daughter. We became good friends, Ruthy and I.

There was only one girl on the seventh-floor closed ward. She must have been near the end of her treatment. She was not a "zombie," but pranced around the hall smiling, full of energy. She was pretty, with striking red hair. I don't think the ward had air conditioning; if it did, it didn't work very well. On hot summer afternoons, I wondered why she always wore long-sleeved blouses and sweaters. A day came that revealed why. There was a big scar on her wrist, and another one and another one, scars all the way up her arm. Each scar represented separate cries, attempts, asking for help.

But there she was on a VA psych ward, alive! Oh Lucy, Lucy…I hope you were able to find the desires of your heart.

The clanking sound from the door's skeleton key announced throughout the hallway "someone" was entering. I always had to look; maybe a visitor for me?

There she was a hallucination? It was Nancy, my high school sweetheart, the dentist's daughter. Nancy, wearing a volunteer uniform, still looking good after seven years.

I don't remember the conversation. Was it a hallucination?

Meals were served in the day room. Because my mouth was always so dry from the liquid Thorazine, swallowing was difficult and I thought I would choke to death! Only soft desserts, especially Boston cream pie, appealed to me.

Once Dr. Johnson, chief of psychiatry, came into the dining area and asked why I wasn't eating.

"Too dry."

He picked up a cookie off my tray, took a bite and returned the rest. "I don't think it's that dry."

182

Maybe my poor appetite was because of eating in the day room. I hated that room! Someone kept playing over and over and over again the song "American woman, stay away from me." What a stupid song to play on a VA psych ward!

As a Naval Vietnam veteran, I wanted an "American" woman to stay, not away, but as snugly close as possible. Only the liquid Thorazine was holding me back from smashing the recording!

And guess who recorded "American Woman?" One of Canada's best-known bands, The Guess Who.

Liquid Thorazine therapy had to include one-on-one sessions with your psychiatrist and group therapy sessions.

My psychiatrist on the seventh floor was Dr. Mier. He was, as a first impression, a foreigner (Australian?), a long-haired hippie with a soft, slow, accented voice and always smoking.

The sessions with the psychiatrist were in a small room with a large wall mirror. First, since I was so heavily medicated, the mirror was insignificant. Soon I would wave at the doctors on the other side of the two-way mirror.

Once while leaving the session, I watched all the doctors leaving their area. I'm not sure if the doctors were observing me or my psychiatrist. The VA hospital is a teaching and research hospital along with Harborview Medical Center, University of Washington and American Lake.

I do know, after the sessions, I felt like I had answered all of the doctor's questions. My mind was completely drained and that was it. Where was the help from the psychiatrist? What about me? Was this just research in liquid Thorazine? The doctor had had his turn, now it should be my turn.

My younger sister Pat visited once. It was right after evening medications. I was "drugged" with liquid Thorazine, lights appeared dimmer than usual and my eyes were blurry, watery, maybe filled with tears.

She came into the large day room. I was sitting on a cushioned chair; my eyes were still blurry, but I could see my little sister coming. She placed a present next to me. It was October 12th, my birthday. She quickly turned and disappeared. No words were spoken. We couldn't find any.

Group therapy works for some people. Group therapy on a closed ward in a VA hospital does not work. No one wants to talk about personal problems when highly medicated. It's hard enough when your mind is clear: As a result there was a lot of silence. The advocates of group therapy tried their hardest to make a success of this failure.

During group therapy patients took turns as secretaries recording the session. The patient before me had taken very poor notes and was told so. My Thorazine had been reduced some and I didn't feel so medicated. For my recording session I wrote down every word spoken during group therapy. After reading the notes before the next therapy session, Dr. Johnson said, "That's good Mr. Olson. But you don't have to write in such detail."

It made me feel good. I was able to write down every word!

The next level of my treatment was a reward to sign out of the locked ward and walk freely to the canteen. With VA pajamas and robe, it was easy to see the difference between staff and visitors. Some of the people in the canteen were normal! Then I always had to return to the seventh floor.

The first weekend pass was with my older brother George. He lived in the Wallingford district, close to the University of Washington. He had found a "fixer upper" old duplex and "fixed it up." This was the first remodeling project, the first of many. The completed duplex was a good example of my brother's skill and ambition.

To be away from the VA hospital! To be away from the seventh floor! To be away from the "locked psych ward!"

It had to be heaven, or close to heaven. We visited awhile, had a small barbeque and it was peaceful. My brother was single. Maybe he had a date; he told me he was going out. He trusted me to be alone in his house. He trusted his little brother.

After several more successful weekend passes and no major problems on the ward, I gained back my freedom as a discharged patient. Of course, there were conditions to agree upon: (1) regularly see a VA psychiatrist, (2) take Thorazine as prescribed, and (3) attend weekly sessions of group therapy for Vietnam veterans at the VA hospital.

I had reached the point where I would consent to anything, even stupid group therapy, just to leave the psych ward and work toward a normal life. Thorazine would not make it easy.

# Chapter 20
# Coping with Thorazine

My level of Thorazine after my discharge from the VA hospital was so high, I could not function in even a close-to-normal lifestyle. I had trouble going to sleep at night, trouble trying to roll out of bed in the morning. My mind wasn't paralyzed, it was so medicated, decisions and thoughts were fogged. I wanted to go to sleep, but I couldn't. I wanted to get up, but I couldn't. All day long I'd lie in a miserable state on a recliner at the boys' home office living room. Finally, Dad said I had to move out of the recliner because people could see me.

I started gaining weight. My cheeks were fat and my stomach was growing larger. I had no drive, no ambition, only a head that I knew was mixed up, tormented. Either by choice or subconsciously, I stopped taking Thorazine.

Within weeks I voluntarily rechecked into the VA hospital. The routine was the same. I only stayed a few weeks. I would swing back and forth through the VA doors for over a year until finally a psychiatrist "saw the light" and reduced the Thorazine.

Another problem developed with the medication. It still left my mouth dry and thirsty. The only solution was beer. Beer was a thirst quencher and eventually helped by numbing all brain cells. The Navy made me a Vietnam veteran and an alcoholic.

The pattern of drinking excessively returned. I was able to function better on a lower Thorazine dose. But straight from the boys' home after work, I'd head to a lounge or tavern to drink beer, beer, and more beer.

While my car was being repaired, I asked Dad if I could borrow the old boys' home pickup truck. The monster Dodge had too many gears to shift, especially for my lack of gear ability. I went out drinking. Coming home, I had trouble shifting, turning through a stoplight. The Lynnwood police noticed. They smelled alcohol on my breath. The usual questions were asked.

"Have you been drinking?"

"How many beers did you have? Can you spread out your arm and touch your nose with your index finger? Can you please walk a straight-line toe-to-toe?"

I told the officers all I needed was some coffee.

"Then you'd be just a sober drunk."

There was no registration in the truck. The dispatcher called the boys' home to verify I had permission to drive.

I must have been on the "borderline" of driving while intoxicated (DWI). The policeman told me to drive straight home.

My father was not happy. He was up when I returned home. I had nothing to say. I had another close call with the Washington State Patrol. After a lot of beer had been consumed, I was overly cautious in my driving. Just before the sharp curve into Bothell, on Bothell Way NE, the state patrol had pulled a car over. As it was a four-lane highway, I passed far to the left to give the state police plenty of room. What I didn't notice was I was going too far to the left and over the center lane. Of course, the State Patrol noticed and pulled me over in downtown Bothell.

"Have you been drinking alcohol?"

Here we go again! I was not inebriated; yes, I had been drinking a lot of beer. Since I was only a mile from home and passed the roadside test, I luckily escaped a DWI citation.

One morning I noticed my car had hit something. Both headlights were smashed, gone. I could not remember what I had done or where I had gone the night before. I had had a complete "blackout." My first. It scared me! My memory was gone.

I slowed down a little after these experiences, even enrolled in a church-related college, Seattle Pacific. The campus was beautiful, though the students seemed involved in their own little groups.

If there was a group of former mental patients, or Vietnam vets, maybe I would have fit in better.

Not one student ever said, "Hi," or asked, "Are you new here?" Of course, I never outstretched my hand either.

After classes in the afternoon, if I had money, I'd drive over the ship canal bridge to the Fremont district. The tavern was better than college classes—beer and pinball machines!

The name on the pinball machine brought back memories from nine years ago, Uplake Terrace, high school, my girl. It was her dad's pinball machine. I could still hear him talking on the telephone trying to "bribe" the Seattle policeman with a bottle of booze to pull my traffic citation.

The beer tasted better and better with each sip. When quarters ran out, I headed home.

Although the Thorazine had been reduced, I hated the little round pills. It wasn't meant for me. I stopped taking them.

The manic highs started out less intense, less common, but still noticeable. Music in the car would always set the spark to fly high with associations.

"Cheer up, sleepy Gene..."

"You probably think this song is about you, don't you? You're so vain...When I kissed the teacher...I believe in angels..."

"Thank you for the music..."

"The angels got together and decided to create a dream come true...they sprinkled moon dust in your hair and eyes of blue...that's why all the girls in town follow you all around...just like me they want to be close to you."

Every phrase would be associated with me or an incident in my life. Sometimes I would hear words that were not part of the original song.

Cameras were still able to see and hear people in the room. A portable TV was placed on top of the console TV in my bedroom so I could watch two TVs at once. It was easy to do, concentration was not difficult and I had twice the viewing power.

Olga Korbut was on the portable TV one evening and the other TV was reporting on Howard Hughes.

It would be interesting to meet the Olympic gold medal gymnast Olga Korbut. What a beauty! I didn't put the prospect behind me.

The console TV was all about Howard Hughes, aviator, movie producer, billionaire and hypochondriac. Where was Howard Hughes? Rumors of his near death were circulating. His life now was a mystery, a secret.

So the TV crews were in Vancouver, British Columbia. Howard Hughes was thought to be living on the entire top floor, a recluse, dying.

After the program concluded showing the great wealth and tragic near-death of Howard Hughes, I asked, "Who is Howard Hughes?"

From the TV came, "You are..."

College "life" soon ended. Without medication the big highs and little lows only brought fear of losing all control of my mind. Once again, I sought refuge as a resident of the VA hospital. Whenever I wanted to block out everything, clear or rest my mind, the VA hospital was the place to go. The revolving door was just as much my fault as it was the VA psychiatrists.' A few weeks and I felt better. A few weeks back on medication.

The summer of '76 was a time to celebrate our country's bicentennial. I had been working both at Arlington Boys' Home and the one in Bothell.

The drive from Bothell to Arlington was thirty-three miles and took about forty-five minutes. The 1–5 freeway northbound was boring. But once off the freeway and heading toward the foothills of the Cascade Mountains, it was country.

Memorial Day weekend was coming soon. I had the weekend off. I wanted to do something special, different, that I had never done before. After looking at several options, I decided Canada was the place to go. Though a native of Washington State I had never visited Canada. The border was so close! 1–5 was straight freeway all the way to Canada, about one hundred miles taking one and one-half hours to drive.

The gas tank was full. Since I had no girlfriend, all I needed was a six pack of cold beer. The beer was cold and I started drinking just outside of Bothell city limits.

From Bothell to Blaine, the US border, this was my special bicentennial excursion. Of course, you must celebrate with drinking beer! Empties on the floor, full cans by your side. I only stopped once the six pack of beer was gone and I needed more.

At the border crossing I wasn't sure what to expect. The border patrol asked only one question, "Why are you coming into Canada?"

I told him, "To visit. I've never been to Canada."

He told me to drive around to the left and go into an office building. I did what he asked.

Inside a person requested my driver's license. Then I waited, and waited and waited.

Finally, my license was returned with an explanation, "You cannot come into Canada because you are too intoxicated."

I could not argue with that. The border patrol must have seen all the empty beer cans on the front seat and floor.

Blue lights flashing in the rearview mirror greeted me as I entered the southbound 1–5 freeway. The Blaine police were waiting for me.

This time, my sobriety tests were more complex. I did not walk a straight line. I did not touch my nose. I went immediately to the police station to blow and blow my breath.

From the tiny city cell I was transferred to the Whatcom County Jail in Bellingham. The jail was actually a large auditorium with bunk beds. I spent most of the time reading newspapers and magazines. I remember nothing about the food or other residents, except it was crowded.

Two weeks were more than enough to be wasting away in jail. My lawyer talked to the judge about releasing me to the alcohol and substance abuse program at the VA medical center, American Lake, Tacoma, Washington. The judge agreed.

The bus headed south on 1–5—a freeway now with familiar sights. Thoughts raced. What's this place called American Lake?

# Chapter 21
# American Lake

The highway ended where a narrow road began—the road to American Lake. Between the trees, the bus moved forward slowly, cautiously. Oh, beautiful evergreen trees! And the green grass was inviting for a roll, a tumble. Evergreen trees and green, green grass. This was the Pacific Northwest I loved!

Leaning my head against the cold bus window, glancing, gazing out, I didn't know what was going to happen. I wasn't sure about this place. I wasn't sure about anything.

Some veterans feared American Lake. They didn't want to go here. And they certainly didn't want to live here. Some who came vowed never to return, ever.

American Lake was more appealing than the Whatcom County Jail. Nearing the sprawling medical center, I was surprised at the old Spanish-style buildings clustered among towering evergreen trees. After the jail, the park setting gave me a sense of peace and tranquility. My spirits were lifted for a moment.

I knew I wouldn't be swimming or waterskiing on American Lake. In my mind I could at Lake Roediger and I did often.

American Lake began in 1923 to care for World War I veterans. Three hundred seventy-seven acres were taken from the eighty-seven thousand Fort Lewis Army Base acres. The VA medical center rested on the western shores of American Lake.

The building for the alcohol and substance abuse program sat apart from the lake and campus of the medical center. Being here and out of jail gave me new hope.

It was a time I was full of energy. The first night I was not tired, so why sleep? Too much going on, too many things to investigate.

The day room had a radio playing. I hadn't heard music for a long time. There was a program called "Songs in the Night.' It played contemporary gospel sounds. I liked it. And it was "night."

The night zoomed fast. I walked around the room observing, checking everything out. I talked to nurses and staff; they talked back. "Songs in the Night" played all night. I never slept.

In the morning a nurse said they wanted to give me a psychological test and a doctor would be in to see me.

The psychological test was the usual, but lengthy. One question caught me by surprise. "Do you look at your poop after going to the bathroom?" What kind of question was that? What did that reveal about your personality?

The meeting with the doctor was more successful than the test. I had met and talked with many VA psychiatrists, but this doctor impressed me from the start. His questions made sense. His answers for me showed some intelligence mixed with empathy. His appearance was friendly and showed class. I liked him, even though he looked like a teenager!

"Gene, I'd like you to come with me to Building Six. All the people there are from Seattle and King County."

Without knowing too much, I consented. I walked across the compound toward the lake with my new doctor to my new "home," Building Six, my residency for the next five months.

I'd forgotten the year was 1976, the nation's bicentennial year. I'd forgotten I was thirty years old. But I hadn't forgotten my history.

Building Six's floor plan was like a duplex without a wall separating the two living areas. Each side was identical. The nurses' station was in the middle. And each side had their own private door entrance, usually locked.

I was placed on the left side. We were patients of "General Sherman," the nickname of our psychiatrist. On the right were patients of "Grismer, the Grizzly Bear," also a psychiatrist's nickname.

When I came to Building Six, I was ordered not to cross over an imaginary line separating the two patient areas. Problem was my area's day room did not have a television, but the day room I was forbidden to visit had one.

The first Sunday the Seattle Seahawk football team was having their very first football game in the King Dome. I desperately wanted to see it! I wouldn't miss it for anything!

The staff was keeping a close watch on me. When I came close to the imaginary line, their eyes were more watchful. I waited until everyone was busy or preoccupied with something else. Then I raced into the other day room and sat down on a chair quickly! No one had seen me. I had made it!

The kickoff was seconds away for the first historical Seahawk football game. In walked two overgrown male orderlies. With one on each arm, I was "escorted" back to my area.

Angry? Yes. But more than that, totally disappointed. Not a very good start for my new home.

It wasn't long before a television was placed on our side in the day room.

The first session with Dr. Sherman was alone in the day room. His questioning was more specific and prodding. I told him, in all sincerity, "I look at this place like American Lake University. I'll do anything for research." I would. But I soon discovered this place was no university.

Anyone observing the medical center couldn't help but sense government research was actively going on.

I did not want to sleep in this building. If I closed my eyes, if I went to sleep, I had no control. I feared if I slept, I might not wake up. Anything could happen. And it wouldn't be good. I feared death!

A black veteran didn't help matters. At night, he sat on the bed, ready to pounce like a tiger. I stayed away, but kept close watch.

Of course, there was no reason to sleep. I was never tired. The only thing to do was walk the halls and any place else that was lit.

The fluorescent lighting at night was bright. As I walked the main hall near the nurse's station something caught my attention. There was a small red button with lettering underneath. The black letters read "PANIC BUTTON!"

I passed the red button and sign frequently. I asked myself, who needs a panic button? And what would happen if I pushed it? Several times I passed by thinking about pushing the button.

I pushed the button! A deep, loud alarm like a foghorn started blaring. An orderly, observing me, grabbed my arm. That was a mistake! I didn't want anyone touching me! Even though he was bigger and taller, I was wirier and quicker. Swinging my arm around his neck fast, I threw him to the floor. With my right arm still tight around his neck, I started punching his face with my left fist. I was mad!

This was not a good way to make friends! The alarm must have alerted every orderly on American Lake. I was picked up and physically carried into the "blue room," a locked room with a dark blue lightbulb on the ceiling.

As my wrists were being tied to the bed with leather straps, several other orderlies were trying to strap my feet. I was kicking as hard and fast as I could with both feet, sometimes hitting a face. Then everything turned into slow motion. Maybe they had given me a shot.

At last I lay spread-eagled on the bed, wrists tied tight with leather straps and ankles tied tighter with leather straps. The staff thought that wasn't good enough. Next came the heavy canvas tarp. It covered the bed completely from my feet to my chin. Ropes were pulled tight from the sides of the canvas underneath the bottom of the bed. It was impossible to move!

When I woke up, the blue light glowed dimly in my face. I tried to move but that was hopeless. To be confined so tight made me more than angry; I was furious!

One thing I could use was my mouth. I started yelling and screaming as loudly as possible.

First on the list were politicians.

F you, President Nixon!" you, Gerald Ford!" you, Jimmy Carter!" you, Henry Kissinger!"

Each name grew louder and louder.

After all the politicians had been drained from memory, I turned my attention to every psychiatrist I had known.

F… you, Dr. Hull! F… you, Dr. Vath! F… you, Dr. Hague! F… you, Dr. Meir! F… you, Dr. Johnson! F… you, General Sherman! F… you, Grismer the Grizzly Bear!"

The yelling and screaming diminished until I could no longer speak. Exhausted, I fell asleep.

In the night a bright light startled me. For a second, doctors and nurses completely surrounded the bed. All eyes focused on me. I went back to sleep.

When I awoke a "guardian angel," Sarah, was sitting next to the bed. She was smoking a cigarette, but that was OK. Some angels smoked cigarettes.

Reaching down with a cup, she gently placed a straw in my mouth—orange juice. Orange juice had never tasted so good! My throat was cooled.

When the drink was gone, she took her cigarette and placed it gently between my lips. I inhaled. She took the cigarette and smoked briefly. Then she placed the cigarette back in my mouth. We shared until the cigarette was gone. She was an angel.

Besides the silence of the blue light I heard birds. Nothing could lock out the chirping of birds, the happy chirping of many birds. They seemed to like my roof.

Time came for the ropes on the tarp to be untied and the shackles taken off my wrists and ankles. It was hard to move anything at first. I was so stiff.

I wasn't completely free. I had the freedom to walk in the small room, but the door was locked, making seclusion. In the back was a large window, not glass, just heavy wire meshed together. Looking through, I noticed a large room or small auditorium. On the wall was a small hole, picked at by other veterans with nothing to do. I stuck my finger in to pull little pieces out. This was my contribution to the hole, the plaster hole.

One afternoon I heard footsteps by the back window. It was a young nurse dressed in a white-skirted uniform coming to visit. She placed a chair in front of the meshed window. As she first sat down, the skirt pulled up, way up, revealing her legs. I just had to tell her, "Your legs are so beautiful." She smiled. Of course she knew I hadn't seen legs for a while.

She was part of nurses from the University of Puget Sound assigned to Building Six. They were all from foreign countries, exchange nurses or nurses seeking recertification.

Jail was nothing compared to the blue room. Being released from confinement was like a resurrection from the dead. I still had some anger and couldn't wait to tell my psychiatrist how I felt.

Deep remorse set in when I saw the orderly I had fought and punched. He had cuts on his face and a bandage on his forehead. I had done it to him. I was sorry, and I told him.

My "angel" Sarah, who was also the head nurse, took me outside for a short walk. The sun and air made my face feel fresh, alive. After confinement all my senses were heightened.

There was a rosebush. I smelled a rose, oh sweet fragrance! I touched it. I squeezed the stem hard. The thorns pricked my hand and there was soft pain. I was alive! Sarah looked and said, "You are a remarkable person, Gene."

I didn't feel remarkable. But I could feel thorns.

As soon as Dr. Sherman set foot in the building, I rushed to confront him. Ranting and raving, I asked why I had had to be confined, and why my wrists and feet had had to be shackled spread-eagled on the bed.

His answers numbed my brain and left me speechless.

"Gene, we don't do that here anymore."

The trip to the dentist was certainly a "trip." An orderly escorted me early, before daybreak, to a building next to the main building. You had to earn the privilege of going through the locked door by yourself.

Sitting in the chair, I became agitated—a lot of lights and instruments everywhere. I wondered where the cameras were.

After examining my teeth, the dentist left and returned with a piece of paper.

"You need to sign this so I can put you to sleep."

I was the wrong person to whom to mention "put you to sleep!" "No, I will not sign it!"

There had been no dentist on my ship and now it had been ten years with no dental work. The dentist said my teeth were very bad and they all had to be pulled. He was a good Mormon and there was nothing to worry about.

I didn't care if he was a Mormon, a Baptist, a Lutheran, a Methodist, or a Nazarene. I was staying awake!

The dentist said there was nothing he could do. I left.

The next morning I had another dental appointment.

Instead of holding a paper to sign, the dentist entered carrying a long, very long, needle. Five shots in my upper gum, five shots of Xylocaine. The numbness worked fast and so did the dentist. He yanked and pulled, pulled and yanked! I left the building with all my upper teeth missing! The Xylocaine helped, but there was still pain.

The next visit to the dentist was a repeat of the last, except this time only half the bottom teeth were pulled.

And finally, after the third visit, all my teeth were gone.

As long as the pain medication was working, my tender gums were bearable, but I could tell the second the medication was wearing off. The throbbing, throbbing all over my gums was excruciating. It hurt! For several days I could not eat or even drink anything.

Slowly I tolerated drinking liquids through a straw. The gums had not healed completely; they were still tender, still painful. At the soup stage, I knew life was improving. And "gumming" food was an art.

As the gums slowly healed, my mind slowly healed. Lithium entered my life. It had only been approved by the FDA in 1970 and now, just six years later, I would be put on" a relatively new drug for manic depression, lithium.

With lithium came monitoring lithium levels to check toxicity. And this meant blood drawings.

She came early in the morning, the "blood lady." I could see her walking down the hallway with a basket under her arm headed straight for me sitting in the day room. Her tone and greetings were always the same.

Please roll up your right arm sleeve and make a fist."

The needle pierced the vein, several vials were filled, and then she disappeared until the next morning.

The first few days were OK. But the every-morning ritual became tiresome.

Days passed and I could not move my right arm or hand. A long dark blue streak was slowly crawling up my arm. The "blood lady" stopped coming.

With my arm and hand partially paralyzed, I was determined to try moving my fingers and eventually my arm. I found a pencil and some paper. I sat at a table; the task proved almost impossible. I could not pick up the pencil with my right hand. I picked up the pencil in my left hand and placed it in my right fingers. They did not want to hold it. It was frustrating. I wanted to write, but I couldn't! On the paper I scribbled as a toddler would. At least there were lines!

A nurse came to take a look.

"Gene, you can do better than that." How I wished I could have!

Soon my fingers were almost normal. In the middle of the night I found paper and a pen and started writing.

*The woods are lovely,*
*Dark and deep.*
*But I have promises to keep.*
*And miles to go before I sleep.*

I held up the paper. The writing was fine. But the words were blurry with double lines.

It was in the day room every morning I met Margaret Osmer for morning news. For me, she was the first original CNN beauty. Actually, I believe it was ABC News. Her style, grace and attractiveness could not be compared to anyone.

As the lithium started working its miracle, calmness, less agitation appeared. The staff recognized this new behavior and permission was granted to leave the locked building during the day.

Also, I was becoming more social, interacting with other veteran patients, one from the air force who used to train guard dogs, another a Native American with an original Indian name. There was an older veteran that reminded me of a host on PBS. And a veteran everyone said had been hit by lightning or a tornado.

The most popular place at American Lake was the canteen. The canteen was in a Quonset hut exactly like the one in which I had stayed several weeks at the Naval Base in Naha, Okinawa.

There was a little store for drinks, etc. And also small tables to sit at to eat and write letters, etc.

The best thing was the free jukebox. There was only one song I would play. I would play it over and over again every time I walked in, 'Take Me Back Again," by Donny and Marie Osmond.

*Oh won't you play for me my favorite melody.*
*Oh let me hear again those wonderful songs.*
*Thinking of way back then, oh how / can remember when*
*We had a lot of friends. Take me back again.*
*Take me back again to my hometown.*
*Want to hear again that sweet old sound.*
*The only happiness I ever found is back in my hometown*
*Just let me walk around through the streets of the town*
*Cause when I feel alone I think about the folks back home.*

Closing my eyes, I could "walk" the streets of Bothell in my mind. There was my bicycle in front of Meredith's Five and Dime. Two quarters from picking cherries were clutched in my hand. On the corner, Crawford's Rexall

Drug Store with the best chocolate cokes around—real chocolate syrup, and a counter with stools to sit on. The homecoming parade down Main Street. The Bothell State Bank, Rich, Vietnam, the "walking" stopped. It was no fun anymore.

To my sadness, "Take Me Back Again" disappeared from the jukebox one day, never to be played again.

Everyone had to go to OT (occupational therapy) once in a while. Building Six had a reserved time and went as a group.

As I filed through the door my eyes were attracted to a beautiful, young black girl. She was a volunteer working with a clay sculpture. Her blouse was unbuttoned just enough to show she was indeed a woman. I was feeling better already!

Looking the room over, I noticed a big, big black orderly standing with his hands on his hips staring at me. I could easily read his mind. "That is my daughter. Don't mess with her!" I didn't mess with her.

On a table were some coffee cups other patients had made. I looked closer at the writing on one cup. "I am not afraid of tomorrow, for I have seen yesterday, and I love today." It was true.

I loved walking around the acres and acres of trees and lawns at American Lake. Although the lake was smaller than Lake Roediger, pleasant memories filled my mind.

Sometimes I'd explore a new building out of curiosity. There were so many buildings to investigate. If the door was unlocked, I figured it was OK to open and go in.

Once in the basement of a building, people were signing a piece of paper and entering a room. I peeked in and saw chairs lined up in front of a portable movie screen. I thought it must be a movie or color slide presentation. Signing the paper like everyone else, I walked in, sat down in the front row. I wanted a good seat.

It was interesting at first, but much too medical. Becoming bored, I got up and left. As I was leaving the speaker said something that made everyone laugh. I don't know what he said, but I can imagine.

The next day my doctor was laughing and said, "Gene, I heard you went to a lecture."

Nothing had said it was for doctors only.

On a sunny day I met a sunny girl, at the blind center building. She was learning how to live blind. Excitement filled her face; happiness echoed in her voice. "I'm going to learn how to live all by myself." She was happy.

Her hair was darker than black. The light from the ceiling spotlight sparkled on the clean, soft strands.

We talked for a long time, mostly about blindness. I wasn't very attentive. I could not take my eyes off of her face. She was so young and so pretty—except her eyes were not pretty.

Another time I met a veteran my age. He had Huntington's chorea disease, a disease of the nervous system. He had not been aware of it until coworkers at Boeing had noticed him shaking slightly. When his wife had found out she had left him. We talked a lot. He had accepted his approaching death, but he could not accept his wife leaving him.

He died when I was at American Lake.

Several months passed and I was feeling great. With this greatness came boredom and a longing to leave American Lake. I was ready. The doctors were not ready.

American Lake was not a maximum-security compound. There were no high walls, barbed wire or a gate. But if locked in a building, you go nowhere. If outside, you can go anywhere.

The city bus stopped at the main building. So it was very easy to board the bus and head for downtown Tacoma.

I had no intention of renting a car, but I ended up at a car rental company, standing around observing people downtown. Someone must have become nervous with my presence since a Tacoma police van arrived shortly. After asking the usual police questions, they opened the backdoor to the van and told me to get in.

The back was empty. No seats, nothing. I lay face down. I wasn't sure where I was going, probably to jail.

The van stopped. We were at the northbound 1–5 freeway entrance.

The Tacoma policeman gave some advice.

"This is the freeway to Seattle. Don't come back to Tacoma!"

Soon a big, red Cadillac convertible stopped. It was a ride; I jumped in. After a while, negative vibrations made me feel uncomfortable. It wasn't because he was black, or was it? When he pulled off the freeway, I made an excuse to get out.

Great! A Pierce County sheriff's car stopped. He asked the usual sheriff questions and I was honest with him about American Lake (mostly) and heading to Seattle to visit my brother. He would give me a "lift."

I sat in front. This time, we were not going to jail.

The conversation centered on Pierce County, Tacoma and Seattle's crime problems. Nearing the Pierce/King County line, the sheriff said, "This is as far as I can take you. Good luck."

A few small rides put me close to downtown Seattle. My objective was still to visit and stay a few days with my brother.

It was dark as I walked on the freeway. The Seattle police stopped, wondering who I was and what I was up to. In the back seat, two of Seattle's finest asked the usual police questions. There was no warrant for my arrest. When I mentioned walking to my brother's house in the Wallingford district, one officer volunteered to have the dispatcher call his house.

We drove off.

Either my brother was not home or he didn't want me to visit. The police said the dispatcher couldn't get a hold of him. We continued driving.

Next stop the Seattle King Dome. The police car's spotlight lit up a clump of ivy. "Do you see that clump of ivy?"

"You can sleep there."

The other officer said, "It's quite comfortable."

I woke up early next morning with three seagulls flying over my head fighting over food. The sun was shining bright with blue skies; I could almost touch the King Dome. The policeman was right, the ivy bed was comfortable!

Wandering downtown Seattle, city of my birth, the concept of time escaped. How many days? I don't know. American Lake didn't look so bad. The food was good. I hadn't eaten for days it seemed. But I needed no rest.

The best idea was to return to American Lake.

It was a mystery how I ended up sitting on the sidewalk at the old Tacoma railroad station. First, I was in downtown Seattle, then suddenly, at the railroad station. The station was abandoned, nobody around. It was peaceful and quiet. The peace and quiet was interrupted by a man flashing his badge, "railroad police."

Another "free" ride to American Lake, compliments of the Pierce County sheriff. It was a general rule if you leave the VA medical center AMA (against medical advice) or walk away, you cannot return. Perhaps my Vietnam veteran status bent the rule a little.

At the main building I had a physical and talked with several doctors and psychiatrists. I was readmitted.

It was back to American Lake and back on lithium.

Building Six was "home" once more. I was "locked up" for several days, until the lithium stabilized me and I promised not to run again.

Toward the last months, my concentration improved. I read four books. Two were given to me by my family. Man in Black by Johnny Cash, and Born Again, by Charles Colson. Autobiographies were my favorites, anything about people. And these were easy books to read.

The other two books I found at the VA library: The Whole Person in a Broken World and Guilt and Grace, written by a Swiss physician and psychiatrist, Paul Tournier. These books were more difficult to read with their emphasis on medical terminology, and they made me think. Casual reading? No. Just a few pages made me tired.

I had just finished reading Born Again when I heard on the TV news Charles Colson was coming to Tacoma. His prison ministry was taking him to explore McNeil Island penitentiary.

The next day a group of people were touring our building. One man sure looked like Charles Colson, only thinner in the face. I was standing in a doorway when they passed by. I'd been thinking about all this prison ministry stuff, so I just had to say, "This place is worse than prison!"

The man I thought was Charles Colson turned to another person and said, "Did you hear that? Olson thinks this place is worse than a prison." Had I given him my name? How did he know who I was?

Five months were long enough to live at American Lake. Dr. "General" Sherman agreed. However, our final session was a little surprising.

"I'm going to discharge you, Gene. We feel we have done all that we can."

American Lake did a good job in my eyes. And in my mind, I could not comprehend the power of lithium, "the salt of the earth," the miraculous gift God had given me this bicentennial summer of '76.

Comprehension would come later. The diagnosis was correct. I was bipolar. I would be bipolar the rest of my life.

# Chapter 22
# Searching for Self-Sufficiency

After hospitalization, especially in a psychiatric unit, it's hard to find normalcy. What is normal? I never wanted to be "just" normal. Normal was too boring. But after all this time of "paranoid schizophrenia" and now diagnosed as bipolar, I felt constrained to hold my feelings and emotions inside. Actually, I didn't have to do any constraining, lithium did it for me.

Leaving American Lake, I still had work ahead. Feeling the best I'd ever felt was an important step. The drinking problem was not resolved. I was just as thirsty as ever. I still loved beer!

This period of my life is most fuzzy and confusing. The events are pieces here and pieces there. It's not as clear or focused as other times in my life.

It was recommended those on lithium drink plenty of liquids. Beer was a great quencher of thirst and an escape route.

The taverns and bars, if they had live bands, became my favorite searching places for companionship. I couldn't dance unless pumped with beer, and then it didn't matter. There were many girls and women, and many stories.

One night of dancing ended up in bed. Nothing unusual, except instead of a "one-night stand," it turned out to be an "eight-month stand."

The Green Lake girl had something; something appealing, something that caught my interest. Her four-year-old son was special. When she asked if I wanted to move in with her, the answer was easy. I had no one. Why not? What was there to lose?

Her sexual vigor and enthusiasm never diminished from the first night. The bed wasn't just warm; it was hot every night, sometimes in the morning and several times on the weekend. Her sexual energy kept going and going, better than any battery.

During this time, I had two jobs. The neighbor helped me get into the painter's union. I did some painting in office buildings in downtown Seattle.

That was fine. But then the union sent me to Todd's Shipyard to paint new ship construction. When I had to crawl down a small hole and paint on my belly, claustrophobia set in and I refused. There went my painting career down with the ship.

The other job didn't pay as much money, but it was more fun and exciting. Even though I was born in Seattle, there were many, many streets of the town I didn't know. As a driver for Northeast Taxi, this would change.

After four months the relationship with the Green Lake girl became legal. Instead of saying, "I do," I should have said, "Maybe later." The marriage lasted four more months.

The wife decided the side effects of birth control pills were too stressful and physically burdensome. She discontinued birth control and soon became pregnant.

It would have been the first time for me to be a father. I was excited and I was not excited. The wife did not want the baby. I had nothing to say about it because it was "her body."

She had an abortion.

"It was pretty easy, just like a vacuum cleaner sucking everything out," she told me.

The next day I walked out. In a few days I was at the King County courthouse filing my own divorce papers. The marriage was over.

It was only a small, one-bedroom apartment in Lake City, north of Seattle, but still a place of my own to call home. Single again.

Driving a cab does not make one wealthy. It was a job, no pressure, and there were always interesting people to meet.

A call to Steve Largent's house in Woodinville made me excited. He had been at the peak of his football career as a wide receiver for the Seattle Seahawks before becoming a congressman and now CEO in telecommunications.

Disappointment set in when I did not meet Steve Largent, but drove his friend to the SeaTac airport.

The highlands were a luxurious, exclusive gated community north of Seattle. The mansions rested in a forest near Puget Sound. The security guards knew their security.

A call came for the Nordstrom's house in the Highlands. I had never known this area existed. My cab fare was "Grandma Nordstrom." At first glance you could not tell she was a member of the wealthy Nordstrom family, longtime Seattle Swedish immigrants. She was just a regular grandma.

All I had to do was mention I was half Norwegian and half Swede, oh "Grandma Nordstrom" liked that combination!

Now, whenever I walk into a Nordstrom store, I always say to my wife, "Did I ever tell you about the time I picked up Grandma Nordstrom in my cab?" She is so tired of it!

Not all cab fares were fun. Sometimes a fare would run from the cab, not paying. Taverns were the worst place to stop: drunks, intoxicated, inebriated, not knowing where they lived.

The scariest call was to pick up a "doctor" early in the morning at the Green Lake Motel. I could not imagine a doctor staying at the Green Lake Motel. It was cheap, rundown and had a reputation for prostitution and drugs.

The "doctor" had two suitcases and looked ill, His skin was orangish-brown, resembling hepatitis, meningitis, "jungle rot" or who knows what? I put the suitcases in the trunk of the cab. The "doctor" was from Los Angeles.

He wanted to go to a Chevron station close to the Space Needle. The gas station was closed when we arrived, but there was one car with a man standing next to an opened trunk.

I opened my trunk and the man took out the two suitcases. I got back in the taxi and as the man was putting the suitcases in his trunk, the windbreaker caught on a handgun in his back belt. Oooops! I needed to get out of there!

The "doctor" did not get off there, but wanted a ride to Capitol Hill, several miles away. I dropped him off at a lounge and couldn't help but wonder if he was contagious.

I usually wasn't happy to have an empty cab, but I was happy now! The drugs and diseases were gone.

Again, early morning, I drove up an unlit driveway in north Seattle. Three young people walked toward the cab, two guys and a girl. Just before reaching the cab, one guy started hitting the girl in the face. It was disgusting, but there was nothing I could do.

My taxi career soured. I didn't want to witness anything like this again. I turned in my keys.

There was a "Cake and Steak House" around the corner from my apartment. I was a frequent customer for the pancakes. The food and coffee were excellent. As an unemployed cab driver, I needed work. This restaurant was ideal because of the location. Even though I had never been a waiter, it couldn't be that hard, so I filled out an application and was hired.

It only took a few days to figure out the menu and become comfortable with the „workings" of a restaurant. Most of the clientele were friendly and easy to serve.

I invited my parents to the restaurant for lunch. Even though being bipolar was new for me, I wanted to explain the best I could what had been going on in my mind and how lithium was helping. I tried. After several minutes, I could tell my dad and mom had no idea what I was talking about. I could not blame them. Some of it I couldn't understand.

Within a few weeks I became night manager. The graveyard shift was no problem since I was used to late hours.

But there were problems in other areas. Within a month or so I was feeling great.

I'm not sure if I ran out of lithium, or like others, the need for lithium was no longer warranted. With little food, no sleep, and mini manic highs coming frequently, disaster episodes lay ahead. It would be the first major manic high since American Lake four years previously.

I'm amazed I almost pulled off this incident. I convinced the staff at the restaurant that the hostess, a grandmother type, was having emotional problems and needed to go to Northwest Hospital for psychiatric evaluation.

When she arrived for work, the plan was to escort the hostess out a side door, into a van and drive her to the hospital.

Everything was fine until the hostess realized exactly what was happening and struggled with resistance. I was losing it! My mind was on getting the hostess into the van. The situation became chaotic. Everyone was running around.

Someone called 911 The King County sheriff asked question after question, trying to figure out what had happened. I became exhausted, placed my head in my hands on the counter and thought about sleeping. What was going on? What had I done? When I told the sheriff, I was manic-depressive and seeing a VA psychiatrist, that was all the information he needed.

"You need to go to the VA hospital, now."

I was hoping the sheriff would give me a "free" ride, but this time I was out of luck. The fourteen miles to the hospital were nothing for a manic-depressive swinging high.

The Pacific Northwest rain poured down with wind in the darkness. The main street of Lake City resembled an old frontier town. The buildings grouped together seemed smaller than I had known before.

Heading south on Lake City Way, I knew directions to the VA hospital: turn through the University of Washington, then walk up to Beacon Hill.

Lightning greeted me as I reached the top of the hill. The rain pounded worse. Off to the right was a Seattle police car parked back on a long tree-lined driveway. For a moment I thought the police car might start up and follow me. But it didn't.

Seeing the VA hospital for the first time in years made me angry. Walking into the lobby, I had no intentions of staying. The recollection is not there, but I must have stopped at my apartment before walking to the VA. I reached into my pocket and pulled out three medals from the U.S. Navy; Good Conduct, Vietnam Service and Operation Double Eagle. In my other pocket was an antique harmonica from my adopted "Grandpa" Chris. I threw the medals and harmonica at the reception desk and ran out.

Walking down Beacon Hill I had to pass the Public Marine Hospital. From the hospital I heard people screaming and crying violently. They were trying to get out! Wanting to get away from the noise I took a shortcut across the grass. Hands r' were stretching out of the ground moving, waving, reaching to crawl out. Further on a person's head was sticking out of the ground. I was terrified!

When I reached the paved road, there was silence for a short time.

A building looked black, sooty, from a fire. Could it be from "the Great Seattle Fire" (1889)? My imagination thought so.

The King Dome appeared to the left. There were more screams and cries, louder and louder! I remembered in the newspaper stories about how the King Dome shouldn't have been built at its present site because of a landfill area. It might slide into Puget Sound!

I feared for the people in the King Dome. I thought they were trapped and everyone was sliding into Puget Sound.

The screams told me there was still a Seattle Seahawks football team. I'm sure the screams and cries were for a touchdown and not, as I thought, people being trapped.

I have no recollection of walking to my apartment, but I made it safely. I woke up in the afternoon realizing the manic high was sliding down. I took two lithium pills.

When I walked across the street to the restaurant, the owner was sitting in the back on the curb. He handed me a piece of paper. It basically said I was forbidden to come into the restaurant, I was dismissed as an employee, and if I came into the restaurant the hostess had permission to call the police and have me removed.

The owner added, "My personal comment is you should seek medical help

This didn't surprise me. However, there was no way I wanted to "visit" the Seattle VA psych ward again.

Within just a few days, the lithium began to stabilize me and I was back to "normal."

While I was collecting unemployment checks, I volunteered at the boys' home. Nothing had changed. Boys' lives were still messed up—boys struggling to find answers, acceptance and love.

"Grandpa" Chris was in a nursing home. He was bedridden. When I would visit, the first question he would always ask was, "Are my barns still standing?" He had built the barns himself in 1930.

"Yes, Chris, your barns are still standing."

How proud he was to homestead in Bothell, to have built the barns by hand in the thirties.

My last visit to the nursing home found the orderlies changing the bedding in Chris's room.

"Where is Chris Rotegard?"

"Are you immediate family?"

"No."

I thought, "Almost immediate."

"He passed away last night."

Oh Chris, yes, your barns are still standing!

He had always told my parents they could buy his six-acre adjacent property after his death. They did, then sold the original Evergreen Heights Boys' Home and built a smaller boys' home on Chris's property.

The boys' homes in Arlington and Bothell were sold as "Mr. O" and "Mrs. O" entered semi-retirement. After unemployment compensation ran dry, I rejoined the payroll.

Moving to a nicer apartment in southeast Lake City was a bright decision. It was on the second floor, one bedroom, with a Franklin fireplace. The fireplace was used almost every night.

My daily diet consisted of a T-bone steak (just dinner) barbecued on the small deck with a hibachi, maybe a green salad, and of course beer, always beer, at least half a case per night.

I never was a breakfast person.

Companionship. What could I do to find a woman?

KVI radio had a "love line" where you could call, record a message, and then it was played on the radio. If a girl was interested, she could call the radio station.

Only two girls were interested in my "message." One never showed up at the designated restaurant, the other one did. She was actually attractive. I should never have said, "You sure are tall!" That was the end.

The Drift on Inn on Aurora Avenue had a sixties-type band. Most nights there was a large crowd. Beer and sex was what I wanted. Cold beer was plentiful. A serious, lasting relationship was not on my mind. It was merely beer and sex.

The future looked bleak for a genuine, lasting, honest relationship. A moment came at a girl's home one morning to shake some sense into my empty head. Her beautiful little daughter, about four years old, asked one question with all the sincerity she knew.

"Are you going to be my new daddy?"

Looking into her eyes, I had no answer.

If God had a girl picked just for me, where was she? I wasn't attending church every Sunday, but I truly believed in a personal God. I wasn't doing anything really bad, just drinking too much beer and sleeping with too many women! Maybe my justification was I had a history of mental illness.

There was one place I did not try, but thought about often, the Little Nickel dateline section in the free ad paper.

I'm too busy to hunt down that special north-end girl, 18–37, weight proportionate to height, no children, believes in honesty and independence/am male, 37, Norwegian/Swede. Work in boys' home. Consider myself "above average" in all aspects. Highly creative and highly affectionate. Would like to meet someone for sharing relationship.

I must confess I prayed to God.

Of course, there would be many replies, my wish. God sent only one.

# Chapter 23
# My Angel from Poland

Hi. I'm interested to know you. My name is Jolanta. I'm 27 years old, 5'7" 155 lbs. (her penmanship), blond, native Polish. I'm a physician (internist) (penmanship again), graduated in Europe. like my job, travels, swimming, sailing, languages and friendly communication. I invite you to answer me. (She then wrote her phone number, scratching out some mistaken numbers and wrote). Excuse fault. If you decide to call, please don't speak too fast. OK? You can write to…With my kind regards, Jolanta.

EXCITEMENT RACED FAST as I read her short letter. This was something else! I read it again. Then one more time. I hesitated. It was the part about "don't speak too fast" if I called on the telephone. It confused me. Why should I talk slow? Was she handicapped in some way? The more I thought about it, the closer I came to throwing the letter into the fireplace. However, "native Polish" and "a physician" aroused my curiosity. Maybe there was something to this girl. I had nothing to lose. It was my one and only letter.

I telephoned. Immediately I knew she was from another country. The strong accent was sharp, but beautiful. We talked about ourselves then asked each other questions.

After exchanging several letters, we finally decided to meet. Denny's restaurant was a couple of miles from where she was staying. She could walk easily. People did a lot of walking in Poland.

Dressed in my best sport coat and nicest tie, I felt reluctance settle in. What was I doing? Was this the right decision? What if she was ugly? There were a lot of "what if" questions, but I brushed all doubts aside.

Entering Denny's, I requested a table so I could observe people coming in at least I would see her before she saw me.

The whole experience was quite stressful. My heart "leaped" a little as each blonde walked through the door not accompanied by a male friend.

*There she is!* I thought.

*No, not that one. Wrong color hair.*

Several long, agonizing minutes passed. Then the moment of anticipation arrived. From a far distance, she was not at all what I had envisioned. Her hair was messy. Her blouse was wrinkled. She looked like she had just stepped off the plane from Warsaw. Of course, maybe walking two miles would do that. But I was not impressed.

It didn't take long, within five minutes, to sense and feel good vibrations beaming from this Polish girl. We talked, we laughed, we talked some more. We ate rainbow trout. We talked and laughed. Two entirely different people from two entirely different cultures, suddenly discovering the joy of a new friendship.

The happy smile, the touch of her hand over mine during some conversations, the impulse. She was indeed unique. She was loving and caring. I forgot all about the messy hair and wrinkled blouse. There was more to see and hear. From the very first, she charmed me.

Her intelligence was obvious. Not only was she almost finished with her medical residency in Poland but she could speak seven languages fluently.

She had vacationed from Poland in between her medical studies to visit the East Coast, but had never been on the West Coast. Then one year she had met a sweet retired lady vacationing in Poland who had invited her to stay with her if she ever wanted to visit Seattle and the West Coast.

Arriving at SeaTac International Airport, her finances were very low. But she had always been industrious. While traveling with a girlfriend in France, she had stayed at campgrounds, hitchhiked, and when money became scarce, found work, once herding sheep for a village lady.

When walking through the University District of Seattle with meager finances, she had noticed three "free" newspapers: a Black newspaper, a Gay newspaper and the Little Nickel that had printed my personal ad. She wasn't interested in the Black paper and she wasn't lesbian. She had called one personal ad and the man had asked, "Do you like to be tied up?" I was glad it hadn't discouraged her from meeting me.

I tried at first to figure out what it was about this girl that made her so much different from other women. I'm sure her Polishness had a lot to do with it…but there was more, something else.

Within a very short time I said to myself, "I'm going to get this girl and keep her!"

I started writing a journal on 12 March 1984. Of course I had started many journals, but had never seemed to keep writing. In the Navy, my journal lasted one trip up the Saigon River. The journal on Jolanta lasted eleven days, until April 2nd. The first entry was a letter to her:

The third time we were together / knew / wanted you for my wife and to spend the rest of my life with you / cannot tell you that now, it is too early, but / have never felt anything so strongly in all my life. Even if you must return to Poland in July / will write you many letters and wait for your return to Seattle…

As we became closer friends, we exchanged letters. In one letter Jolanta wrote:

In fact, I'd like to tell you so much when we are together but (I'm sorry, but I must tell you truth) when you kiss me, I forget about the whole world around. told you what I feel but still is too early to give the name of these feelings.

Jolanta said she was impressed I took her to a family dinner so soon after we met. There was a lot of excitement flying in the air since my family had never met her—and probably because very seldom had a girl accompanied me to a family gathering. I shall never forget my oldest brother's comment as he smiled, "Where did you find this girl?"

A few weeks passed and discussions on marriage entered the conversations, at first as something abstract, then as personal. The "gamble" might be more for us, two entirely different cultures and two newly made friends.

With the situation still tense in Poland, under Communist thumb at the time, we thought the Seattle immigration office might have some advice. An appointment was made.

We explained the situation; we had just met, but cared deeply for each other and fell "in love." And Jolanta had only three months left in her three-year Polish medical residency. She wanted to complete the program.

"Should we just become engaged, or take the chance and get married?" I asked the immigration officer.

He was quick to respond, "I suggest that if you are really serious about it—get married. It might be hard for Jolanta to leave Poland. It's still a Communist country."

Several days later while sitting on the edge of the bed I read her a poem I had just composed, "Will You Marry Me in May?"

Will You Marry Me in May?

Will you marry me in May?

Please give an answer in April someday.

I do not promise money or gold.

Only to love you with a heart never cold.

Will you marry me in May?

To Poland —Jolanta Olson—is the only way. Two people together might sometimes fight but love can always light up the night.

Will you marry me in May?

Please give an answer without much delay. I count the days when I will hear "Yes I will," from my sweet dear.

Will you marry me in May?

I can see no other way.

I'm not afraid to say how I feel

My affections for you are genuine and real

We stand in love always together So be my wife now and ever.

Will you marry me in May? This is all I have to say.

When I finished reading, I told Jolanta there was no need for an immediate answer.

One day went by…no answer. Two days went by…no answer. Then three, four days…no answer. Finally after two weeks she said "Yes, I will marry you! But you have to stop drinking beer."

I know why she took so long to answer. When I had moved to the apartment in Lake City, I was still drinking beer heavily, half a case a night. I was throwing the empty cans in the spare closet to recycle later. When Jolanta first saw the apartment, she opened up the guest bedroom closet and hundreds of beer cans came flying, cascading to the floor!

Didn't they recycle in Poland?

Alcoholism was so severe in Poland, causing such sorrow and pain.

I never had another beer.

Our marriage took place at my parents' house in Bothell, at the small group home for boys. A staff member was a licensed minister and officiated. Jean, the lady who had invited Jolanta to America, stood as a witness. The wedding consisted of the minister; bride, Jolanta; groom, me; my parents and Jean. Six people all totaled, just the right size!

It was hard to believe, meeting someone so fast, falling in love even faster. And now married, on a honeymoon, heading south on Interstate 5, in a little blue Ford Courier pickup with a beautiful, sweet Polish girl as a new wife.

Instead of taking the freeway to Disneyland, Highway 1, though much longer, sounded like an ideal route. The scenic, twisting highway along the Pacific Ocean coast was too beautiful to resist. What a magnificent drive! We never regretted taking extra time.

The greatest thing about the honeymoon (besides the obvious) was we planned nothing. We were free to do anything. We were free to go anyplace. We just jumped in the little Courier pickup and started driving.

Since we had a late start out of Seattle, Salem, Oregon, would be our first night as Mr. and Mrs. Gene Olson.

The huge sign with red lettering could not be missed from the freeway, MOTEL 6. Economical on our budget, and at least it was clean.

"What's this?" asked my wife as she pointed to a coin clot by the bed.

She had never seen a "pay for vibrator bed" in Poland. We put a quarter in, rolled on the mattress, and soon felt cheated of twenty-five cents. But it was a good laugh, vibrations!

The night was not a laugh. The night was perfect!

The next afternoon we finally arrived at the north ern California coast. Even though a cool May wind was blowing, the beautiful Pacific Ocean was so inviting.

The beach at Santa Barbara was irresistible, so much so we had to stop and explore the area.

Though I was lying on a blanket with only summer clothes, the weather didn't matter, I was still in heaven. I glanced over to see my new, beautiful bride next to me. She had unbuttoned her blouse and was ready to take her bra off! I asked, "What are you doing?"

She said, "I'm putting my bathing suit on!"

I answered, "But..."

Before I could finish, she said, "But what? Do you see anyone on the beach?" True, we were the only ones on the beach! Of course I'm no prude. But this was my cute, innocent, Polish girl, unaware of American culture and practices. I had a lot to learn and I would. She was a good teacher.

The drive continued along Highway 101 with magnificent views and small coastal towns. We always stayed at "economical" motels, but soon learned to "check" the room before agreeing to register.

As the little pickup slowly descended into Los Angeles, there was no mistaking we were in Southern California. With all the smog, the sun appeared to be wearing sunglasses. The bright day was turning darker. Traffic increased and so did the humidity.

With dusk approaching, we drove several hours before finding a decent motel between Long Beach and Los Angeles. The next day driving to the "beach" at Long Beach, my bride pointed out, "Hey look, there's a UFO." From a distance it did look like a "UFO," but it was only the Goodyear Blimp!

Whenever I see a blimp, I must remind my wife of the approaching UFO! Of course, her reply is, "I knew it was a blimp all the time."

It was great to honeymoon at Disneyland in early spring. Crowd not too bad, weather just perfect. The fun and excitement of being a kid again! We had so much fun, fun, fun! It definitely was a small world after all.

We would return in later years with my wife's brother from Poland, his two young sons and our two young sons.

After Disneyland had exhausted us, it was time to head north, to Seattle, the Pacific Northwest and trees. As usual, the return trip is always the longest, always the most boring. And it was true for us. The weather even turned cloudy and rainy.

The only bright event took place crossing the California desert. We passed an army convoy with an open truck full of soldiers coming back from weekend maneuvers. Due to high humidity, my Polish bride was wearing a low-cut, revealing tube top to relieve the heat. As we passed, one soldier caught my wife's eye, or should I say my wife's "top" and soon all the soldiers were yelling, waving and whistling. Not at me!

Poor "Weekend Warriors!"

Being a Navy veteran, what could I do but smile and thank God she was MY wife!

All the way down to Disneyland and all the way back to Seattle a few cassette tapes were played over and over again. By the time we reached Seattle, my bride was "sick" of Abba's "You Are the Dancing Queen" and I was "sick" of Polish folk songs and Russian marches!

We returned to Seattle as husband and wife knowing our love would be separated. We lived each day to its fullest realizing the separation was soon. As fast as we had fallen in love, we were saying goodbye.

SeaTac International Airport is fuzzy. I recall not feeling well. Maybe it was physical, maybe psychological. It was probably a little of both. And sadness, I'm sure.

We convinced ourselves three months was not a long time. In three months we would be together again. Three months was only ninety days. But it wasn't fair for newlyweds.

There was dead silence returning to the apartment. My little Polish bride was gone. No laughter came from the bedroom. The king-size bed was empty. She was nowhere. It was the loneliest time of my life.

I kept repeating in my mind, "Only three months. Only three months." As days passed, I felt very alone, like in the Navy standing watch. I envisioned my wife at Denny's, the first time I had seen her, the first time we had kissed, the first of everything.

Sometimes I had to stop. Memories could hurt.

Just as I had convinced myself three months was not a long time, tragedy struck. Major, major tragedy.

Jolanta returned to the hospital in Lublin to resume her residency in internal medicine with only three months left.

The medical director at the hospital was not happy. "Since you traveled to the United States, we are changing your program. Your residency program will be extended for one year."

Those Communists! How could they do that?

The news hit hard. I was devastated! There was no way I could wait a year for my wife's return. Three months was OK, but not twelve. That was impossible! The letter writing started.

# Chapter 24
# Second Honeymoon – Polish Style

Sorrow is like a bad cut on a finger. At first, the pain hurts, throbbing, blood all over. When a bandage is applied, the bleeding stops. Tylenol reduces the pain. Soon the cut is healed, the bandage is off and all that's left is a scar or no trace of the wound.

For my sorrow "cut," the only bandages were letters for healing. I wrote a letter every day to my wife in Poland. They were not just short notes, but long letters about the days' activities and days of longing, aching to be with her.

The letters from Poland were sometimes few and sometimes short. It took me a while to realize she was studying and working at the hospital. It was hard to write so many letters and receive slow replies from someone you loved desperately. But my sorrow cut was healing slowly each day.

We decided halfway through our separation, six months, that we should have a second honeymoon in Poland. I had never met my new mother- and father-in-law. And of course, being away from each other so long was becoming more than unbearable. Now I had something positive to look forward to.

It was about fifteen years since I'd been on a plane, from Japan to the U.S. to be discharged from the Navy. Although I had some hesitation about flying alone, nothing could keep me away from my beautiful new bride, nothing.

Thanksgiving 1984 was a time to be grateful. As a bipolar on lithium for eight years, my mind was at peace; I was newly married and now headed to Poland for a second honeymoon. At last, I would be with my wife, even though for a short time.

The flight from Seattle to Chicago's O'Hare International Airport was delayed one hour. Consequently, the connecting flight from O'Hare to John F. Kennedy International Airport was missed. My only alternative was a flight to

LaGuardia and a bus ride to JFK. All the luggage arrived in LaGuardia except the important garment bag.

Waiting at JFK's Pan American Airlines check-in, all ticket holders for LOT Polish Airlines had assembled. Now I was the foreigner in Polish country. Everyone was speaking Polish, loud and fast.

LOT Polish Airlines did not have a gate or concourse from which to arrive and depart. A huge "people mover" resembling a large square box moved the passengers from Pan American gate to the Lot airliner parked away from the terminal.

Walking into the "people mover," I had my first glimpse of Polish self-urgency. Everyone was pushing, shoving, and elbowing with desperation.

I thought, "What's wrong with these Polish people? Don't they know everyone has an assigned seat?"

They acted like the plane seats were first come, first served. And nobody wanted to be left behind!

The Polish stewardesses were very attractive and spoke with authority. An elderly man received a stern verbal "lashing" for trying to store extra packages improperly. Everyone had extra carry-on packages and luggage. Even a priest was carrying a large box containing a complete model train set.

Blankets and sock slippers were handed out. The airplane seemed small; there was no leg room and sleeping was impossible. Maybe it was the anticipation of seeing my wife, but I think having my knees in my chest made for a very long, uncomfortable flight.

As the plane was descending, the pilot informed the passengers, in Polish and English, we were close to Warsaw International Airport. Hot towels were passed out; a refreshing wash after a long flight.

However, my excitement was delayed several times. The airplane would almost come to a complete stop midair, like brakes on a car, then speed up. First, I thought we were landing. Then a slowdown, speed up, slow down, speed up. I wondered if we would ever land!

Finally the wheels squeaked on the runway, and the passengers started yelling and clapping. The man sitting next to me said, "Well, I didn't think it was that good of a landing."

The old Warsaw International Airport had no gates or concourse area. Passengers disembarked down ladder steps and walked to the terminal.

Polish soldiers wearing Communist light green uniforms started walking toward the debarking steps. Stepping off the airplane, I noticed two soldiers had a firm position at the bottom of the ladder. One soldier started running fast up the ladder toward me. That didn't look good! An elderly lady in front had difficulty coming down the steps with her bags and the soldier came to her rescue. The soldiers were very friendly and courteous to all.

During martial law there had been several confrontations between the police (feared Zomos) and the Polish soldiers. The soldiers did not like the brutal tactics the police used on the Polish citizens. In general, soldiers were more liked than police.

Walking, staring, I headed with the crowd to an old building. It was hard to believe, I was actually in Poland! Inside the building, I was not prepared for the „welcoming." Only a long, glass window partition separated the passengers going through customs and the Polish public coming to meet everyone.

Little children had their noses pressed against the window. Adults were waving frantically trying to get people's attention. Then I saw her, front window seat, smiling, waving. Six months I had waited for this exact moment! She was still beautiful.

A customs official walked by the line speaking in Polish. I asked the man next to me, who was Polish but could speak English, what he had said.

"You have to exchange American money into Polish money at the window before you enter customs."

I exchanged some money and was given a receipt as proof to show authorities wherever I went.

Standing in line again for the baggage check, I couldn't keep my eyes off the window and my sweet wife. I didn't know what to expect in this foreign Eastern European country. But I was happy to have a beautiful guide and excellent interpreter.

The customs agents were asking people to empty everything out of their suitcases. Even some women's purses were closely inspected; every item was taken out.

I tried not to show fear or nervousness as I handed the customs official my passport and visa.

Sternly, not looking my way, he asked, "Do you have any gold to declare?" I thought for a second.

"I have some jewelry for my new in-laws. But it's only fourteen-carat gold-plated. I don't know."

Louder came the same question, "Do you have any gold to declare?" I quickly answered, "No!"

He stamped my papers and passport and never opened one piece of luggage. He pushed a button to the locked door and immediately I was in my baby's arms hugging tight, embracing, not wanting to ever stop!

Jolanta introduced my new brother-in-law and a friend who had driven his taxicab from Lublin. Everyone had been sleeping in the taxi since six o'clock in the morning. The flight from New York had been delayed four hours.

I didn't realize how I exhausted I was, without sleep, until I sat down in the taxi. There were so many things I wanted to say to my wife. And I wanted to talk with my brother-in-law, Jurek, but the energy was gone.

I tried to stay awake during the four-hour drive to Lublin. It was hard. The eyelids did not cooperate.

In Poland, the first thing I noticed about the buildings was how old, drab, cement-brick gray they were, colorless and just run down.

My wife's comment was, "The government owns the buildings. Inside where people live, it is very nice."

There were not many cars on the road, just a lot of people walking, bundled for the freezing weather. Often a horse-drawn cart would appear mostly carrying wood or coal.

The cluster of buildings scattered throughout the countryside aroused my curiosity. I thought they were farms with barns.

Jolanta was quick to say, "They are small villages."

Even though the weather was freezing cold outside, downtown Lublin was bustling with people. Like all Polish cities, Lublin had an old town and a new town. The old town was old and the new town was old.

It was easy to tell the government owned my parents-in-law's building. The outside had never been painted, still dirty gray from original construction. Windows were broken, even one to the main entrance door. The mailbox inside was metal from World War ll. There was no elevator. Up three flights of stairs was my in-laws' apartment, reinforced with four locks on the door.

Having watched Polish people at Kennedy Airport say "farewell," I was prepared to greet my wife's parents with a kiss on each side of the cheek.

The apartment was a very small one-bedroom, older with a warm Polish atmosphere.

As I was still experiencing jet lag, food was the furthest from my thoughts. Jolanta's mom had other ideas. The dinner was beyond belief! First a giant bowl of fresh beet soup; that was a meal in itself. Full. I could have stopped there. But no, next the main course, meat, potatoes, vegetables, and several things I had never seen before. I tried my best to eat everything, but could not. Plus, the eyelids again did not want to cooperate; staying awake was difficult.

My wife's job of interpretation was poor, actually worse than poor. I always had to ask, "What is your mom saying? What is your dad saying? What is your brother saying?" And then, "Tell your mom this. Tell your dad this. Tell your brother this." It was frustrating!

Bedtime came. Though extremely tired, I didn't want to sleep. Six months alone and now together.

The old hide-a-bed in the living room was next to the paper-thin bedroom wall of my wife's parents. I would not sleep alone tonight.

There was love, quiet love.

Since it was November, the weather in Poland was snowy, miserably cold and windy. On the first day we took a bus to downtown Lublin. I had not anticipated the Polish winter and had come dressed for Seattle rain, a tan corduroy sport coat and black slacks,

My wife was concerned I might freeze, but had a suggestion:

"Why don't you wear a pair of my pantyhose?"

What? I couldn't believe my ears. "Pantyhose!"

She was persuasive. I didn't want to be a crossdresser in Poland but this was a matter of survival.

Walking downtown I was warm and happy to be wearing pantyhose. I didn't feel feminine at all.


The first stop downtown was the post office. I wanted to send word to my parents I had arrived safely in Poland. The telegram office resembled an old train station

My wife waited in line as I stood to the side.

Lines would soon be a common sight. Long lines for meat. Long lines for bread. Long lines for chocolate. Long lines for shoes.

If you wanted anything you had to stand in line. Some line people didn't know what was at the end, but if it was long, there must be something good.

Soon commotion erupted behind the telegram counter.

There were frantic searches in the garbage cans, underneath the counter, clerks were running around, confusion everywhere.

My wife came and whispered "Put out your pipe, there is no smoking here."

I had just lit up my pipe and the smell had made people think there was a fire. Borkum Riff, Bourbon Whiskey tobacco did it, not me.

Walking the streets of my wife's hometown was a sharp contrast to walking the streets of Seattle. Now, firsthand, I was learning more about Polish culture and customs.

Little by little I would learn and catch glimpses of the little Polish girl who was now my treasured wife.

Jolanta's first role of playing the doctor had been a medical experiment.

She was given her Teddy bear a water shots. Unfortunately, the Teddy bear was stuffed with a straw and her mom had to take all the straw out to dry.

Before Jolanta had entered school, she was always trying someone to read her a book. Her dad was falling asleep reading the book and her mom was too busy.

Finally in desperation she said to herself "If no one is going to read to me, I will teach myself to read."

And she did, one letter after one letter, then put them together.

When she was four years old her mom took her and older brother Jurek to a pediatrician. He asked Jurek to read and he has some difficulties.

Jolanta's mom said "My daughter can read it "

After she read the part of the chapter, the doctor said "She probably has this memorized"

The doctor got a newspaper and she started reading. The doctor asked her to stop and asked all his colleagues to come and listen to her.


Once in school her hunger for reading increased. There was a local library within a walking distance from the appartement building but after reading all the books in the children section she asked her mom to take to the Old Town library. You had to travel by bus to get there.

"Why did you come to this library," librarian seemed puzzled, "there is one closer where you live."

"I have read all the children' books in that library" she answered

I don't know if the librarian believed her. But I do know she is still reading and reading and reading.

Chocolate in Poland was scarcely available, usually during Christmas.

Once being a small child, she wanted the piece of chocolate so bad...She found a small brown stone and put in her mouth then prayed and prayed that it will turn into chocolate.

It was known fact between children in the neighborhood that all Americans were very rich. They were so rich that, that when got bored with their cars – they would leave them on the side of the road with the keys in them. Whoever came walking along and needed the car would just jump in and drive away.

When she was seven years old, she had spilled a pot of boiling oil on her leg.

She was in the hospital for 30 days with no visitors – including parents – allowed in the hospital. That was due to hygiene regulations.

The teacher come every day so she doesn't miss school and they were other kids. Still it was lonely time and a lot of physical pain from dressing of the deep burn.

The two and half mile walk towards east was still cold and snowy. The pantyhose kept me warmer and the wife felt pity because she has bought mt a warm stocking cap.

Soon the bitter cold outside will be forgotten.

On over 600 acres, the Majdanek State Museum was a Nazi concentration camp.

It was created in 1941 as a POW camp and ended up second to Auschwitz extermination camp.

Trying to explain Majdanek and our "walkthrough" is difficult.

The difficulty lies in the remembrance of historical Poland, WWII, pain suffering, sorrow, evil and death of millions.

The entrance to Majdanek had a small fence made out of black jagged metal. The entrance gate read "Majdanek Monument to Struggle and Martyrdom, a symbol of tragedy, hope and victory"

The monument resembled a gigantic stone resting on two fat legs.

In front were steps leading down to a flat cement surfaced pit or ditch with ragged rocks stacked straight up along the sides.

Standing there, you felt the rocks could bury you.

From the monument there were steps leading down to an old brick path.

The path was straight and led several miles to the crematorium and Mausoleum, barely seen in the distance. Within a mile or so the camp compound appeared to the right.

Guard/watchtowers, electric barb wire fences, barracks and buildings-just small reminder of what is was. A death camp.


We were the only ones at Majdanek until a car came speeding around the corner, a distance back, just before we reached the mausoleum. Four men in black leather overcoats jumped quickly out of the car. I thought, 'Now what?"

The mausoleum was larger than the Majdanek Monument, but made from the same stone material. It had a small dome and wide band around the bottom. Under the dome was a high mound of dirt, ashes and tiny bones, from the graves of murdered prisoners.

The inscription on the mausoleum read in Polish, "OUR FATE IS A WARNING TO YOU."

While you stood in silence, the dome-covered dirt stirred your imagination. Who were these people of scattered bones?

The four men from the car were now standing reverently, silently next to us. One man placed a bouquet of flowers on the ledge, a group picture was taken, and off they went back to the car as fast as they had come.

The crematorium was next on our walk. It was an old structure beaten by weather and frozen Polish winters. My wife opened the door to a dark, cold room. Walking slowly, we saw the brick ovens as shadows in the dim light. There were no windows. The camera flash lit the room for a second.

Around the corner it was lighter, with a small window. Then we saw the iron gate opened to the oven, revealing a metal stretcher with black handles to slide in one body and slide out, empty. More ashes, more tiny bones.

There were more buildings. We stopped.

The walk back to town was long and cold.

My father-in-law showed us the Lublin city newspaper the following afternoon. There was only one picture in the entire newspaper on the front page. It was a group picture taken at the Majdanek Mausoleum. The men had been journalists and newspaper executives from Czechoslovakia paying respects. I could be identified by the stocking cap. Jolanta was partially hidden, lucky for her, since the only way she could get time off for the second honeymoon was to request sick leave from the hospital.

The bus ride downtown was short, but always packed, especially during winter. I still can't figure out the fare system. First you bought a ticket at a kiosk. When entering the bus, front, side, or back, you inserted the ticket into a notch on a pole where it was stamped. But no one, not even the driver, ever checked the people's tickets. Seems to me a lot of people were riding "free."

From downtown we walked to the Lublin Castle. Part of the castle was built in the fourteenth century and remodeled Gothic style in 1823–1826 for use as a prison.

To enter the museum we had to place slippers over our street shoes. The Polish and foreign paintings, along with folk art and weapons display made me want to linger several hours longer.

Then we came to an old table. My wife told me "The Legend of the Devil's Hand."

The year was 1637 in Lublin. An old widow lady was called to court by a rich and greedy neighbor. He claimed her house and property were his.

He paid the judges money to rule in his favor.

The desperate widow cried, "Even the devil would give me more justice than you'

Suddenly a strong wind blew the doors of the court open. Four men dressed in black judges' robes walked through the door.

They said, "We come from the highest court to review this case." And they ruled in the widow's favor.

The other judges were terrified, but did not protest.

The main judge of the four said, "As proof of this verdict we leave a stamp."

He put his left hand on a stack of books at the table. Smoke rose up and filled the room. The four judges left quickly.

People in the court became frightened. As the smoke cleared, they saw the hand had burned through the books and even the table top.

You can see the table with a burned hand today on the display in the museum.

Our next adventure was a six-and-a-half-hour train ride from Lublin to Krakow. The station swarmed with activity and of course, long lines for tickets. With the old Polish trains, piercing whistles and steam shooting out the sides, I felt pushed back in time. Was it the forties during World War II?

The train bumped along with a rhythm uniquely its own. Soon we were in the countryside passing farmlands and observing storks feeding on grass or perched in nests on small electrical poles. And I had thought storks only delivered babies! What were they doing in Poland?

Small towns and villages appeared and disappeared. People were always walking, a few on bicycles. The time on the train flew fast.

Krakow had witnessed more Polish history than any other city in the country.

Most major cities in Poland were ruined or severely damaged during World War ll. Miraculously, Krakow's wealth and old architecture from different periods was saved. And no other city in Poland had so many historic buildings, monuments land works of art, totaling 2.3 million.

Hotel accommodations proved to be a problem. It was my wife's idea to speak Polish when seeking a room, since Polish people should have preference. Right? Wrong!

First hotel, "no vacancies." Second hotel, "no vacancies." Third hotel, "no vacancies." Fourth hotel, "no vacancies," but they knew a place that rented out bedrooms.


The next night my wife was still persistent, Poles should have priority in hotels. It was the same. First hotel, second hotel, third hotel, all "no vacancies."

"OK Jolanta. Now it's my turn, in English!"

First hotel, "Yes, we have accommodations."

My wife did not take this very well, feeling discriminated against, and me, the American, getting special treatment.

Two unforgettable sights of Krakow had to be the "Cathedral of the Kings" and Church of St. Mary.

Stepping down a small ladder, we saw beneath the "Cathedral of the Kings" were tombs of Polish kings, queens, national heroes and famous Polish poets.

The ancient tombs had elaborate carvings, crucifixes and miniature statues. One tomb of a king and queen, side by side, had a baby's tomb resting on top of the king.

Being cold and tired in the late afternoon, my wife suggested we stop at Church of St. Mary to rest and meditate. To describe the church as "beautiful" says nothing. The outside and inside must be seen to grasp the grandeur and sacredness of this Polish church.

Sitting down, we saw there were many side chapels, shrines, and important works of art. The silver and gold sparkled. A large crucifix from the fifteenth century and Gothic stained-glass windows from around 1370 were just part of the treasures that made this church remarkable, one I can never forget.

From the highest tower, the famous trumpet call, the Hejnal, was sounded hourly. The call was unfinished, in memory of a medieval trumpeter shot while sounding the alarm of invaders. The Hejnal was broadcast live by Polish radio daily at noon. I heard it.

The two-week second honeymoon, Polish style, two short weeks, seemed like it was over just as it was beginning. After the fun and joy of being together, sharing every minute, loving each other, I wanted to stay, but reality said there was no other way except separation again.

There were no tears from my eyes at the airport, but inside, my heart was crying.

# Chapter 25
# Together Again, Finally

I returned to Seattle with emptiness. My life was empty without Jolanta. I wasn't sure if I could survive another six months alone. It seemed like an eternity. I was hoping the next six months alone would be better than the first six months. At least I could say I had been to Poland. At least I had met my father- and mother-in-law. At least I had spent "some" time with my wife. At least I was still married, if that's what you wanted to call it.

I continued writing a letter every day. Disappointments came frequently when no mail arrived from Poland. I still had difficulty realizing Jolanta was working hard at the clinic or hospital and had little spare time to write.

Once in frustration I saved seven letters for a week's writing, circled a number on the back of the envelope and mailed them all on one day. I don't think Jolanta saw the numbers when she read the letters and thought Polish mail was just slow.

Another time in anger I sent Jolanta a very harsh and cruel telegram. I accused her of being "cold," "unloving" and "uncaring" because she wasn't writing many letters. This surprised her and it surprised me. I had never thought I could send a telegram so vicious.

It was good for us both. Jolanta had more empathy for my loneliness and I understood more what she was enduring. After "steam-blowing" with the telegram and talking with my wife, the days and nights became more bearable.

At this time, my parents decided to retire from the boys' home business. The decision made me happy.

After starting in Bothell during the fifties with over ten foster children and now directing two boys' homes with thirty-three boys, they had dedicated over fifty years of service to others.

Over the years, some boys' home graduates have been successful and some have been failures. A few of the success stories are a computer whiz, a football player for the University of Washington, a policeman, a Navy SEAL and the list goes on.

Unfortunately, a few of the failures ended in prison, a few became addicted to drugs, and one committed suicide.

The discussion of retirement for my parents brought up the question of what to do with the boys' homes. They asked if I would like to continue working home and working there. It was difficult not to become emotionally involved and to just stay clinical. It was not a touch decision to tell my parents, "I don't want to."

A position opened up at Northwest Center Industries. This was a large complex just north of downtown Seattle and south of Ballard, a Scandinavian community. The center was non-profit and served a large population of mentally and physically handicapped people.

First, I worked as a staff member in the janitorial training program. It was a good program for handicapped people to learn a skill, graduate, find regular employment and maybe even live independently.

The offices of Blue Cross and Blue Shield of Washington and Alaska, Mountlake Terrace, WA, had a contract with the center. The restrooms had to be cleaned, toilets, sinks, mirrors; wastebaskets emptied; floor mopped and waxed. All desks in work areas had to be dusted, wastebaskets emptied, carpet vacuumed, tile floors mopped and waxed.

The staff would do time studies for each task. We timed ourselves on how long it took to clean a toilet, clean a mirror, empty wastebaskets and mop, etc. The handicapped people were expected to eventually do the task according to the time study. Some were able to, others could not. The amount of work performed was reflected on their paychecks.

I enjoyed helping and training the workers. It was different than working at the boys' homes.

There were four on the staff. Three were gay; I was not. I tried to "tune" out the gay conversations for a while, but soon it was too much. I didn't care to hear about all the "cute" boys at the steam baths in Pioneer square and their escapades.

Eventually, I transferred to the sheltered workshop. The clients were more severely handicapped. The tasks were easy, but did require some manual dexterity.

One contract was assembling writing stationery. First, sheets had to be counted to a specific number. Second, someone counted the envelopes. Third, the sheets and envelopes were placed a certain way in a gift box. Finally, it went to the shrink-wrap machine. The staff performed quality control throughout the process. Each worker was given credit for the amount of work performed. The higher the performance, the larger the paycheck.

Another contract was easy, well, for most. There was a contract with the Port of Seattle. Sometimes freight would come in, like toys, with no "made in Japan" or "made in China" stickers. The worker would be paid by how many stickers were placed on each individual piece.

Again, the incentive was Friday's paycheck. This was their occupation.

Sometimes a parent's motive to help is so persuasive it's hard to say no. This was the case when my dad came up with an idea he thought was great.

Instead of paying rent every month, literally throwing money out the window, my dad's idea was to buy a used mobile home. It would be like a small investment, as he would be selling it later. He found one that was nice and was sure I would like it also.

As we both looked at it, I was not impressed. But Dad put on the pressure. "You can't expect to start out in a mansion."

Under the circumstances, my wife in Poland couldn't see it. I did explain everything in a letter with hopes she wouldn't be too surprised and liked Dad's idea.

The owner/manager of the mobile home park was leaving in several weeks for Israel and asked me to be the manager. He would be gone for about a year. I agreed. I'd never been a mobile home park manager, but it couldn't be that difficult.

At first, the three hundred dollars (for rent space) seemed like a pretty good monthly wage. After the first month I had my doubts. The clubhouse had to be kept clean and rented out. All rent checks had to be collected from the box and late people had to be hunted down. Then all money had to be written down on a deposit slip and taken to the bank. All of this was very time-consuming.

And I can't forget the "hazardous" duty. While I was dumping trash in the dumpster, a big dumpster, the lid flew down and hit me on the nose. It hurt so, so bad and wouldn't stop bleeding; I had to drive to the VA hospital emergency room. Just another scar.

All this time, I was still writing daily letters to my wife. The last six months did not seem as terrible as the first six months. I had come to the conclusion there was nothing I could do to change anything. I was powerless to speed things up.

As time approached for my wife's return, problems arose in Poland. Those Communists!

I didn't have all the specific details, except my wife was having problems with the American Embassy.

Now there was something I could do! I wrote a letter to Senator Dan Evans explaining my frustration and anger. He promptly replied back that he would look into the situation.

Through all the pressure applied by Senator Evans, the "red" tape and my wife's difficulties ceased. When she last went to the American Embassy in Warsaw, she was treated like a top diplomat. She felt like other Polish people were mumbling, "Who is this lady? Why is she getting special treatment?"

One of the greatest moments in my life was getting a collect call from my wife at

Chicago's O'Hare Airport. She had made it to the United States! Finally, soon in my arms at SeaTac Airport! The excitement climbed higher and higher!

As we kissed and hugged at the airport, I never wanted to be separated from my wife again, NEVER!

As predicted, Jolanta was not too thrilled with the new living arrangements. We both agreed it would only be temporary.

Suddenly the bed was a lot warmer in the evening and in the morning. Love and loving are never cold. Once again, we were husband and wife, happy to be!

My wife was a physician in Poland, but not in Seattle. She had to start all over and jump the hoops for foreign medical graduates.

Plus, if we wanted a family, time was slipping. I was thirty-nine and Jolanta thirty-one. We devised a plan. After she received her physician assistant license, we would have our first baby. When she met all the requirements qualifying her to enter a residency in internal medicine, we would have another baby. This would be tough. Jolanta would have to study hard since foreign medical graduates had special exams to pass.

First, she would study for a physician assistant license. As she was waiting for the license, she did volunteer work at several free clinics in downtown

Seattle. Once my wife had volunteered there, she enjoyed the challenge of working with "down and outers" in this free clinic. She was hired. Not only did they get a physician assistant they also hired a Polish doctor.

The mobile home was sold and we moved into a very nice apartment in Des Moines, south of Seattle. Although we were close to the airport, after several days the jets landing never bothered us.

True to the plan, Jolanta became pregnant. The PA was going to become a mom and I was going to be a dad!

Rejoicing filled our hearts as preparations went forward to welcome the new baby. As my wife's tummy grew bigger and bigger, the joy in our hearts grew bigger and bigger. We wanted a baby and we were ready.

Bus service was better in the north end of Seattle so we moved to an apartment in Mountlake Terrace. Also, the hospital where our baby would be born was close by in Edmonds.

As delivery time neared, I was doing my best to be sympathetic with my wife, but sometimes I failed.

My wife invited her brother from Poland to stay with us during the birth of the baby. Polish hospitals have strict regulations on visitors none. Nothing had changed since my wife had been in the hospital as a little girl.

Her brother Jurek was excited and anxious to see his sister and the new infant on his first visit to the United States.

Early, early in the morning my wife said, "I think it's time."

Rolling over, I grumbled, "What are you talking about?"

"Call the doctor. My water just broke!"

Standing at the hospital reception desk, seeing the water dripping around my wife's shoes I was convinced, her water had broken.

All morning nurses and doctors were in and out of my wife's room. I was working on timesheets for my group of handicapped people so they would be paid. Everything around was quite boring.

Then some action started. Because of the baby's position there would be a C-section delivery. And I would be able to be in the delivery room!

There was a sheet up around Jolanta's head to conceal the delivery. I sat in a chair next to her, talking and giving some reassurance. There was a large mirror in back revealing most of what was going on. As the doctor's knife made the first incision, I'm glad I saw only his hand and not my wife's stomach.

The whole procedure was fast and easy. As the doctor pushed his hand in to find and grasp the baby, I shivered! Then this little light purple newborn let out its first cry announcing his arrival. To experience the miracle of birth is an experience beyond words, beyond explanation, but never to forget.

As the nurse gently laid him on the table for cleaning, he quickly flipped his legs high up. She responded, "Oh, this one is going to be easy to change diapers on."

She wrapped my new son in a blanket and placed him on my lap. The unspeakable joy, pride, and happiness filled me to overflowing. This was my son! And his mother, I'm sure, looked on, feeling the same.

In the haste of the early morning water break and hospital confusion, I had forgotten all about calling my parents and telling them the baby was on its way. As soon as I could, about ten minutes after the birth, I called with the news. My mother said, "Why didn't you call sooner?" I thought ten minutes was pretty soon.

Jolanta's brother was surprised he could just walk in and see his sister in the hospital room. He had a big smile on his face when he entered and saw Jolanta with the baby. We were happy he could share these cherished moments with us.

Whoever said a new baby was a disruption to the family probably was not thinking about ours. There was a disruption for us, a beautiful disruption.

I wanted the name "Gene, Jr." for our son, but Gene cannot be translated into Polish. However, Paul can be translated as Pawelek. So we settled on Gene-Paul.

A few months later I started reading some baby books and articles on early child development, and then I stopped. I read a very interesting three-book review in the Sunday newspaper. What interested me with the subject of babies sleeping.

The first expert author in his book said if a baby is crying at night, just let the baby cry until asleep. Don't pick the baby up.

The second author said if a baby is crying at night, pick the baby up, give reassurance, put the baby back in the crib and let him go to sleep, even if the baby starts crying again.

The third author said if a baby is crying at night, pick the baby up and rock it until it goes to sleep.

After reading the review on these three books, I realized doctors and experts had a wide range of opinions. Who was right?

The last "idea" of the mobile home had not worked. However, my parents came up with another plan that sounded better. They had remodeled the downstairs of the tri-level former boys' home into a mother-in-law apartment. They wanted us to live there, "rent-free," so we could save money for a down payment on a house. It sounded good. Naturally, their new grandson would be closer, real close.

The remodeled mother-in-law apartment was a job well done. It had three bedrooms and a fireplace in a large living room.

When the baby was six weeks old it was decided I would become a stay-at-home dad. I was still working at the center for the handicapped, but as a physician assistant, my wife's salary was much larger.

At six o'clock in the morning I would be my wife's taxi and take her a little over a mile to the Bothell Park and ride. Around four in the afternoon I would pick her up.

My dad loved his grandson dearly. He had to hold him and talk to him several times a day.

Jolanta was becoming a little exhausted when the baby had trouble sleeping at night. Years later, she would say it was a mistake to have the baby's crib in a separate bedroom. The crib should have been right next to her bed.

I took my title STAY-AT-HOME DAD very seriously. The diaper business started out rough, but each time it became easier. The bottles, the drinks, the baby food, everything was down to perfection—oh, the crying and sleeping needed some work.

As I was shaving one morning, I saw my son in the stroller watching every move. I looked in the mirror. I asked myself, "Why am I shaving? Am I going to work? Do I have a boss to impress?" That was the last time I shaved. Well, I did have to shave each time we flew to Poland. And after fourteen years of a Viking beard, the wife asked me to please shave. She was tired of it. I should have caught the hint when she asked me to shave before traveling to Poland.

We invited my in-laws from Poland to visit and see the baby. It was their first visit to the United States. We were a little concerned about them making all the flight connections. Everything worked out OK. My father-in-law made several bookcases and stained them. Going to the lumberyard, he picked out the most expensive wood. I told my wife it was cheaper to buy one from the store. Her remark was, "True. But look how much fun he's having."

Our house fund had reached our goal for the down payment on house. We had only looked at a few houses when an ad in the newspaper caught my eye. A three-bedroom rambler in Lynnwood with fireplace, one-car garage, reasonably priced, just what we needed.

We met with the builder. He had been renting the house for several years and now wanted to sell. Jolanta liked the house as much as I did. We talked it over. The old saying about sleeping one night on any major financial decision sounded good. But we didn't want to lose this one.

As we were signing the earnest money agreement, someone was knocking at the door. The builder said, "I'm sorry. The house has been sold." Music to my ears. We had our first house. Soon it would be our home.

The house was located close to the Lynnwood Park and ride, being convenient for Jolanta to bus to downtown Seattle. The buses were larger, more comfortable and stayed on the freeway all the way.

My parents stopped by frequently. In fact, Dad had to stop by every day. The love for his grandson was immeasurable. After playing in the house, they would go for a ride in the car. The most popular place was the fountain at Floral Hills Cemetery.

Foreign medical graduates had higher and stricter requirements than American medical graduates to enter residency programs. Tough medical and even English exams sometimes had to be repeated.

There were periods when my wife was constantly studying medical books or listening to medical cassette tapes. Her best study position was walking. I knew when to talk and when to shut up.

The studying, the walking, it all paid off when she finally passed all examinations and met all requirements to enter a residency program in internal medicine.

Time now for family planning. With our son four years old, we were ready for another baby. And my parents were ready for another grandson. Besides, PA license—a baby, qualify for residency = a baby.

Mom and Dad, of course, were thrilled to hear another baby was on the way. Even though they had eight grandchildren, one more would still be a special gift.

The telephone call was one I dreaded. Dad had fainted or slipped on the porch steps and was rushed to the hospital. We also rushed to the hospital.

Sitting in bed, he didn't look or feel well. He didn't have to say anything, but he did.

Over ten years previously my dad had had triple bypass surgery. I don't recall him being in the hospital, maybe I was also in the hospital.

Now my dad needed another bypass surgery. Because he was seventy-six years old, the operation was more critical. The doctors felt he was strong enough for a successful bypass.

The family gathered together just before the operation.

Dad was lying on his back in a stretcher. Everyone had a chance to talk, to wish the best.

I knew Dad was heavily medicated. I leaned and kissed him twice. "One kiss is from your grandson."

He softly said, "Thank you," and smiled.

According to the doctors, the bypass was successful. The success was short-lived. Dad never regained consciousness.

I had been home thirty minutes after visiting Dad at the hospital. There had been no change. The telephone rang. It was my brother-in-law. Dad had just passed away. I cried. My Dad was gone. I cried some more.

I don't know if it was the birth of his grandson or something else, but over the last few months Dad had changed. He had tried to get closer, putting his arms around my shoulder and showing signs of affection. At first it had made me feel uncomfortable, until I sensed it was his love for me.

We never agreed on everything. I know I disappointed him many times. His legacy will live on with his children. For me, his legacy was love, an unconditional love. I pray my children can say the same.

There was a memorial service at the Aurora Church of the Nazarene.

Burial was at Floral Hills Cemetery. I wondered what my little son was thinking. Maybe his grandfather could take him to the fountain I didn't know how to tell him his grandfather couldn't take him there anymore.

Life had to go on. My wife was pregnant and growing bigger each day. She had to have her interviews for residency programs before anyone "noticed" she was pregnant and discriminated against her. And she had to have the baby before her program started at the medical center. Plus, before I took over responsibilities, the baby had to be older than a week. Timing was important.

For residency programs the entire United States was our territory. We sent out letters to medical centers for applications, places where we'd like to live.

It didn't surprise us to read in one letter, "Our program is so competitive that the chance of a foreign medical graduate being accepted is slim." In other words, don't bother to apply.

Then, happily, positive applications started arriving and soon interviews were being arranged.

Mixing work with pleasure, taking a short vacation during the interviews, sounded like an excellent idea. After discussing several alternatives, and since it was nearing winter, the Amtrak train was the best choice. Our four-year-old son jumped with delight.

We waved goodbye to Mom at King Street Station in Seattle; the train headed north and then east over the Cascade Mountains. Puget Sound looked different, beautiful, as the tracks hugged the shoreline. The mountains and wilderness, my favorite trees…how happy I was not driving.

It was a bright idea to reserve a family room to accommodate my son's playing, everyone's sleeping and the wife's morning sickness. We had a private room and windows on each side. My son soon found the excitement of how to open the doors between cars. We walked to the end of the cars and back, to the end of the cars and back, over and over again.

The first interview was at University of North Dakota Medical Center at Fargo. The flat Montana fields were getting boring from the train, so it was a relief to sleep in a hotel room.

My mother had been born in Ryder, North Dakota. I still had some cousins living in the area. We all met for dinner one night and talked family.

While my wife was at the interview, I walked with my son downtown. The only real excitement in Fargo was standing on the sidewalk waiting as a freight train passed. It was a long one, to the amusement of my son.

Next stop was Minneapolis/St. Paul. A physician my wife worked with in Seattle had relatives living there. Her father met us at the train station and drove us to another daughter's house. We were their houseguests several days.

Again, not much to do during interviews, but good relaxation and good walks to the nearest McDonald's.

From Minneapolis/St. Paul, Amtrak rolled into Chicago passing through the "poor side" of town. We transferred to the "Hoosier Express" heading for

Indianapolis, Indiana. This express was definitely not made for comfort. The seats were hard and barely reclined. If you wanted to sleep, good luck!

The train pulled in next to the Hoosier Dome and soon a taxicab picked us up for the University of Indiana. The university had made reservations at the convention center on campus. It was very elegant. Too elegant for me!

The interview went well. One thing my wife liked was all the hospitals, the university hospital, the VA hospital and the public hospital, were within walking distance of each other. She still didn't have a driver's license. U.S. roads were not like Polish roads.

The train ride back to Seattle was the longest and most tiring. No night motels, just train, train, train. Plus, the only family room available was a handicapped family room. Putting a pillow on the toilet by the window was not the most comfortable way to ride, but survivable.

The highlight was when the train made a brief stop at Minot, North Dakota, close to Ryder. This was where my mother had been born! I had to step off and stand on the ground of Minot, North Dakota. I wanted to be able to say, "I was at Minot!"

My son started yelling, "Dad, the train is leaving!"

I jumped onboard, satisfied.

When the time came to discuss all the interviews, I remember distinctly saying to my wife, "I really don't care where we go. I just want to leave Washington State." I still missed my dad.

The residency programs worked on a matching system. You sent in your first choice, second choice, etc. The medical centers would also give their preferences. The final matches were published in the USA Today newspaper classified section.

What excitement! All that little print! And there it was, Jolanta's first choice was a match with the University of Indiana Medical Center.

The next priority was to sell the house. We had been lucky to buy the house just before there was a dramatic increase in sales. Boeing was booming and the Seattle area economy was bursting.

There was no reason to list a high price assuming to come down if it didn't sell. We had a few months deadline, so selling quickly was important.

The house sold to the first person to look, even before the hole was dug for the "For Sale" sign. Thank goodness a herd of people didn't have to tromp through the house.

Amazingly, we had lived only a short time in the house and walked away with over thirty thousand dollars.

After closing all details on the house, we flew to Indianapolis to meet with a real estate lady I had been working with over the telephone and via mail.

Our realtor gave us a guided tour of the Indianapolis area and answered all our questions.

We knew mostly what we wanted in a house. This made it easy for the realtor and easy for us. From nine in the morning until six-thirty in the evening, we viewed around twenty houses and narrowed them down to a final four. (The Final Four NCAA Basketball Tournament was playing in Indianapolis.)

Surprisingly, my son enjoyed house hunting, going directly into the children's rooms and checking out the toys, stuffed animals and books.

Relaxing back at the "economy" motel room, we were exhausted. So many houses, so many areas, so many floor plans, we hoped the final four were the right houses.

It was Saturday night and Indiana was playing Duke in the Final Four Basketball Championships. My wife and son were sound asleep, so I turned on the basketball game without sound. Indiana made a basket. From the room above came thunderous clapping and yelling. Duke made a basket. From the room above came boos and foot-stomping on the floor. Looking toward the beds, I saw everyone was sleeping soundly. But after several minutes I couldn't take it!

"I'm sorry, Sir, but we don't enforce the quiet time until ten p.m.," snapped the desk clerk.

Oh, that did it! When I was through with her, explicitly showing my outrage, it took only three minutes to clear the upper room of sixteen university students partying in a room designed for two.

The flight back to Seattle concentrated on decisions made and alternatives if "something" went wrong before closing on the house. Time was a major factor.

Time also was a major factor in the birth of our second baby. Because the baby and my wife were so healthy, she was going to have a second C-section—maybe once a C-section always a C-section—and the sympathetic OB doctor would deliver two weeks early. Two very important and crucial weeks. Our plan was working, almost perfectly.

This time, my wife invited her mom and dad from Poland to stay with us during the birth of the baby. I did not stay in the delivery room, but waited in the lounge with my son and in-laws. As soon as my second son, George, was born, they called me to the hallway and a nurse came with a little bundle. He hadn't been washed yet, so tiny and just gorgeous! After a brief moment the nurse rushed him away.

Soon everyone was in my wife's room with the baby snuggled tight. There was a video camera ready taking in the newborn, the smiles, the laughter and the Polish gibber-gabber.

Now we were a family of four. More diapers, more bottles and more love.

The future looked bright. I would be saying goodbye to Washington State and greeting Indiana. One thing was certain; we would be together as a family. Three years in Indianapolis. I was soon to be a "Hoosier."

# Chapter 26
# Becoming a Hoosier

"Moving can be fun and a pleasurable experience," the moving consultant said. Oh sure!

There are not too many native Washingtonians left. But I am and always been proud to say "I was born in Seattle, Washington." I lived in the Seattle a of my life. Now by choice I was moving to Indianapolis, Indiana.

After several moving companies came to the house for "consultations," of my life. Now by choice I was moving to Indianapolis, Indiana.

After several moving companies came to the house for "consultations," a company based in Indianapolis was chosen.

I was a little native to think the moving van would arrive on time, at a twelve o'clock. After some frantic telephone calls, the van backed up to our four hours late. The driver was grumpy, angry and very unprofessional. Having driven up from Indianapolis, he was just given notice to pick up our belongings. He came to the door, he never introduced himself, he never wore a belt. Every time bent down, which was quite frequently for a mover, half his butt was, well, the picture. He wasn't going to take the car because it wasn't on the invoice. He wasn't going to take the mattress and box spring because they weren't in the box. Something new to me. He wasn't going to take the large glass-covered because they had to be glass-wrapped.

After more frantic calls, most everything had been settled. By ten o'clock the van slowly moved down the road with my car following behind. It was too dark to load the car, so they were going to load it at the warehouse.

My stress level increased, wondering if we would ever see our car and personal belongings again.

The earliest our contract read for delivery was June twelfth, the latest June to twenty fifth. My wife was starting her residency at IU Medical Center on June twenty-fourth. We didn't have much faith the moving van would be early, but there was always a slight glimmer of hope.

It was raining when we left Seattle. It was raining when we landed in Indianapolis.

Our new home was just as beautiful as we remembered. Only one problem—it was completely empty.

As soon as the neighbors heard we had noting in the house, little things began to arrive. On neighbor gave us a cooler filled with ice. Another brought over a portable color television and a small radio. And besides, bringing the fruits and groceries, the realtor gave a big cushioned chair for my wife to feed the baby. What a blessing for the one chair.

Sleeping on the floor was not as bad as I had anticipated, just a few sore muscles in the morning. But the empty feeling of nothingness was hard to accept. My wife called it the most depressing part of the move. We called the toll-free number every day to check the progress of the van. And every day we hear the same thing, "June twenty-fourth," the day my wife started her residency.

No one had told us about tornados. No one had told us about thunder/lightning storms. No one had told us about ice storms. No one had told us about floods. Indiana weather would tell us!

We arrived only a few days before a storm hit Indianapolis. Everyone was asleep on the floor except me. The wind and rain smashing against the windows kept me awake. The forceful sounds were frightening.

I turned on the television. There was a map on the screen and a message from the announcer, "this is an emergency broadcast...there is a tornado watch...and there is a tornado warning...What was this guy talking about? What was worse, a tornado watch or a tornado warning?

Then he said, "Everyone should be undercover."

Well, we were undercover, there was a roof overhead. Then I thought if the tornado came may be the family should be in the crawlspace under the house. It was large enough to stand up in, with a long steel beam running beneath the house. It would have been the perfect refuge except water was gushing over the sides at a rapid pace.

The next day a neighbor explained to be undercover meant to go to the center bathroom, where there was no window, sit in the bathtub or under the sink covered by a blanked, etc., and brace for the worst.

A few days later while we were grocery shopping, an announcement came over the PA system. Please do not leave the grocery store. A tornado has been spotted a mile away.

I imagined the roof falling, shelves and cans crashing, bottles shattering all over. The best place to be was the paper aisle.

We made it home

I did not believe that the moving van would arrive as promised at 9.00 a.m. when my son yelled at 9:10, "Here comes the moving van, Dad!" I was surprised.

It was my first day with our two-week-old son and he was protesting quite loudly—no Mom!

I decided to put him in the entrance to the guest bathroom so he would be out of the way and sleep better in the stroller.

As soon as the first mover walked down the hall, the baby woke up. This time protest was ten times as loud and vigorous as the one for Mom. Why was he crying?

Next thing to check was the diaper. Right, diaper full. Even still, crying and crying.

I had planned to check the numbers on all boxes, furniture, etc. to make sure all items were accounted for. Unfortunately, the baby had other ideas…crying hands were indeed full. Fifty percent of all items were checked off.

The driver assured me everything was unloaded and nothing lost. Of course I had to sign a waiver stating I did personally check off all content. My wife called from the medical center and rejoiced with me as I said the van had just unloaded our earthly possessions. Now maybe we could unpack and start a "somewhat" normal life.

When the last mover left the house, the baby stopped crying. Peace at last. That evening we went back to the master bedroom to see how nice it looked. As I sat down in the corner, the mattress moved like a teeter-totter. Great bedframe was set up for a king-size bed. Our mattresses were queen. How come the mover not know the difference? And then to be so lazy as not to change it. Ste I quickly took the bed apart and made it right. A bed is important.

Three days later as my wife was putting the baby in the crib, the spring fell through. Luckily, my wife was there to catch the baby. The movers had left screws out of the bracing frames, causing a gap to misalign the rest of the crib

Slowly, each day boxes were unpacked and saved for the next move in three years. As the final boxes were emptied, we realized some things were missing like carton marked for the kitchen—some dishware, the answering machine. A box with medical books for the wife. Most of her medical books had not made it. And lastly, we couldn't find the baby carry basket. Several days later, we found a box for the kitchen—some Polish dishes and a knife set.

Another frantic call, this time to Seattle. Then another call back to Indianapolis. What was going to happen? Who knew? If I had thought it would do any would have written a letter to the company CEO expressing my dissatisfaction and frustration. I almost did.

About a month after the movers departed, the company called saying they had located our missing cartons on the van in Connecticut. Soon we would be completely moved.

The first day of residency, Jolanta asked to be picked up at the hospital at five pm

We were right on time. No Jolanta. We could wait a little. Six pm, no Jolanta. Seven p.m., no Jolanta. The boys were getting restless! Eight p.m., no Jolanta! Nine p.m., yes Jolanta! Four hours of anticipation!

The decision was made then—Jolanta would call from the hospital when she needed a ride.

My wife's favorite saying is "You do what you have to do." The three years of driving morning and evening to the hospital proved that statement true. I had no choice. It wasn't such a pain; at least we had two trips out of the house. I did what I had to do.

Life was happy and running smooth. The deck from the kitchen door entertained the boys. The fenced backyard with swings and a slide also kept the boys busy.

The winter snow and ice storms did not compare to the mild winters of the Pacific Northwest.

A problem came just as we prepared to go to the airport for Poland. Looking puzzled at our youngest son, my wife said, I think he is limping. He was just starting or just trying to take small steps.

It was too late to see the pediatrician. Besides, they were supposed to check a child's development, making sure everything was OK.

In Poland, my wife quickly contacted a pediatrician also a friend, X-ray would have to confirm the diagnosis, and everything pointed to a dislocated hip.

He was not to walk at all. But he wanted to walk and run so bad! The three-week vacation tested my patience.

Back in Indianapolis, the x-rays clearly showed the hip was dislocated. There definitely would have to be an operation. It would have been easier on my son and the family if the pediatrician had found out earlier. I was upset but my wife claimed sometimes those things happen.

Riley hospital for children was nice, but in reality, no hospital in nice. We brought our son in the early morning. As the medication wore on, our son became sleepy. We kissed him. The nurse took him, now out of sight.

In the hallway my wife started crying. We embraced tightly. Tears came to my eyes. There was such a feeling of helplessness, no control and fear. Did it matter that the surgeon was the chairman of the department of orthopedic surgery? Did it matter that Dr. De Rosa was better than the best when operating on children? No, that was our boy!

Sitting in the waiting lounge, to us a minute seemed like an hour. A nurse stopped by. The operation was half over and everything is going fine.

But the best news came from the surgeon. Dr. De Rosa said everything was successful. He talked about everything he had done, including what screws he had used. From the first moment we had met the doctor we were impressed and trusted him.

And now we were happy in the good news.

Our son's recovery was speedy. My wife took some time off to be at his side and spent four days and night with him never leaving his room.

Upon release from the hospital, adjustments had to be made. Our son had cast that went around his chest to the bottom of his right leg. A special child's chair let him lie on his back or stomach. He had to be carried to the back seat car and strapped in with special seatbelts.

Later the cast would be cut smaller and the difficulty of everyday life eased.

When the cast was finally removed, after some therapy, my son could walk normally. The operation was a success except for one permanent mark, a scar on his thigh. He doesn't remember much. Later in his life he would ask, "Dad, how did I get this scar?"

Naturally, my wife had to invite her mom and dad from Poland to Indianapolis. It was a long flight for them, but they enjoyed seeing their daughter and the rest of the family.

Painting the deck was a project easy to put off. I had several days before her parents arrived and was eager to continue. I have several cardinal rules for painting

1. Don't spill the paint container;
2. Don't ever drop paint on cement;
3. Don't leave streaks;
4. Don't use too much paint; and
5. Do a professional job.

I have done a lot of painting in my lifetime. Some rules, unfortunately, have broken. If I had a choice, I would paint by myself without any "help."

Now in came my father-in-law. He was so eager to help paint the deck. As I was so eager not to have him paint. Jolanta's persuasive charm changed everything She was right; it was only a paint. But only paint can sometimes go where paint be removed or painted over.

I must admit my father-in-law did a good job painting. My mother-in-law a pest at times, trying to supervise her husband. There was only one problem. the end of one deck railing he painted past the end and onto the painted aluminum siding. There was no way I could wipe off the dried paint. The colors were close, still a noticeable difference.

I was upset, until I remembered it was only a paint.

My wife had one last two-day examination as a foreign medical graduate The place, Des Moines, Iowa. Looking on the map, it didn't seem too bad driving from Indianapolis to Des Moines. The old Ford Escort might make the trip.

The drive along the Mississippi was intriguing. I thought I saw Huckleberry Finn and Tom Sawyer floating on a raft, until I realized it was 1994.

Immediately upon crossing the state line there was no mistake you were in Iowa. The farms and fields are luscious green. The most green I'd seen since the Pacific Northwest.

We arrived in De Moines early evening, happy to have survived the long journey. The hotel room was adequate, but our fast-food budget almost killed some of us.

I did a lot of walking/strolling downtown with the boys. The domed solarium brought delight with the many plants and birds flying around.

The exams were over. I had preferred to drive in the daylight, but now it was dusk and Jolanta had to be at the hospital the next day.

We had driven easily from Indianapolis on Freeway 74 during the day. The only real problem was the interchange to Highway 80 just before the Iowa border. The map had shown three different routes crossing the Mississippi River. They had all looked about the same distance. I had picked one and we had made it OK.

When we left Des Moines, it was dark. After several hours driving, a thunderstorm hit. The lightning struck so close to the car on each side. Then the rain poured. The visibility was near zero. Creeping along, if only I could see better the fear would cease. The lightning did help the darkness.

The sign said Indianapolis but I had no idea where the road was or if I was going in the right direction. I guessed and eased right. I could not see the highway. God only knows how I made it.

Many miles later in the pouring rain, I still had trouble seeing. I said to the family, that's it. We're pulling off to the side of the road.

If I couldn't see the road, how could I pull off? I pulled off the road to the shoulder, hoping it was the shoulder. I could just see a semi-truck smashing into our little car.

People must have had Midwest common sense and stayed off the freeway during the storm. We only saw one car, actually a pickup truck, with a blue light flashing on the dash board trying to get around my slow driving.

The rain eased. I still wasn't sure if we were headed in the right direction. Then peace and relief, as a big well-lit sign announced "Indianapolis." We had made it! We were heading home.

Even now, while driving to the ocean or Seattle, someone has to ask, Hey Dad, remember the drive to Des Moines?"

The three years flew fast, speeding. Jolanta passed all medical exams with high marks.

Driving every morning and evening to the hospitals through sometimes tiresome, was insignificant. "You do what you have to do." First thing whenever she decided to practice medicine, she would do what she had to do and get a driver's license!

Besides the long, weary hours of residency, my wife's only other complaint "I wish when the doctors talked to me, they would look into my eyes and not my breasts."

I didn't say a word as I looked at her breasts.

Searching for a place to practice medicine was more enjoyable than searching for a residency. Mostly Jolanta flew around the country. The entire family did to Vancouver, Washington. Several miles from Seattle, it was a small town on the outskirts of the Columbia River.

I loved southwest Washington! I loved the Columbia River! It was up to interviewers and up to the "Sergeant-major" (my new nickname for the wife) as to the final outcome would be. Of course, I did have "some" say in the decision.

The final interviews were over. The decision was made. I was happy!

# Chapter 27
# It's Vancouver, Washington, not Vancouver, British Columbia

There is a T-shirt around that reads: "It's not Washington D.C., it's Washington State. It's not Vancouver, B.C, it's Vancouver, Washington."

My wife joined a small group of physicians in Vancouver, Washington. Southwest Washington was our new home.

Soon Dr. Olson would become a partner in a medical clinic and later also serve as chairman for the department of Medicine at Southwest Washington Medical Center.

It was wonderful to return to Washington State, land of my birth. All I would miss from Indiana was the sunny hot summers reminiscent of South Vietnam and the South Pacific. Nothing could compare to Washington green

And in Vancouver there was a Colombia River and nearby Mount St. Helens. We would walk almost every weekend on the cement path built along the river. The drive to Mount St. Helen was spectacular and we never tired of the Mountain View from Johnson Ridge Observatory. I could see St. Mount Helens from Vancouver every day. Well that's not exactly true some days were cloudy.

The wife's first mission was obtaining driver's license. Yes, she had no problem except she would not drive on the freeway for several years. I was still required to drive to Portland for medical conferences etc.

Driving from Portland over the I-5 Bridge to Vancouver, I always glanced at the freeway shoulder where years ago I had searched for cigarette but while hitchhiking to Seattle. Halfway across the bridge where I had stopped in admiration, I saw the glorious Colombia River had never changed but I had.

Vietnam Veterans of America found a real Huey helicopter. The placed it on a steel post with a slant. It sat on the corner of the Salmon Creek American Legion as a memorial to all. It has special meaning to me. It's the same type of helicopter my school friend Rich Worthington was piloting when he was killed in Vietnam.

Every time, every time I pass the helicopter, I felt the presence of Rich; his spirits around.

After several years in our first house, it was decided to find some acreage build a house with a mother-in-law unit for my mom. She was in her eighties driving on the freeway, still a Norwegian, and liked the idea of living close to family.

Driving around for several weeks, I found the perfect place in an area Pleasant Valley. In a pasture there was a homemade sign showing two parc land for sale. I like the two-and-one-half acres. The owner had just gone through a divorce. His ex-wife's settlement was the Appaloosa horses; he had received property. His loss was my gain!

It was fun watching the road be created—the bulldozer pushing dirt for the foundation, and deciding exactly what our new house would look like.

Mom was busy designing the mother-in-law unit, where the walls would where the fireplace should go.

While the house was being built, we rented an apartment near the Vancouver mall. The boys enjoyed the swimming pool and I enjoyed running to the prevery day to check out progress.

Jolanta thought it would be an excellent time to invite all her family from Poland to visit. The family of four would suddenly jump to nine, in a two-bedroom apart

But that was OK. The house was ready to move into. My wife's two strong nephews could help move belongings in the little Ford Ranger pickup from storage new house.

The sounds at night were identical to Bothell, crickets and loud frogs croaking. Except here a new sound was added, howling coyotes. And they could howl!

The house was built as far away as possible from 159 Street. This meantabout two acres of grass in the front to mow on the riding mower.

My son liked to mow until he ran over several baby rabbits. It was an ugly scene. Another terrible accident also happened in Vancouver. A grandmother on a riding m o w e r backed up over her small grandson. He didn't die, but was cut badly.

I was cutting the front grass when a TV news crew stopped. They asked if I had heard about the mowing accident and wanted to interview me about riding safety.

The last time I had been on TV was the high school mock political convguess it was again time to be on the news!

While I was sitting on the riding mower with a camera rolling, they have asked basic questions on riding mower safety, etc. I certainly had a lot of experience and thought the interview went well.

"We'd like you to drive up toward the house so we can film you on the mower."

I anxiously awaited the evening news from Portland. It would be great to be on TV!

The segment started on riding mower safety. The anchorman was sure doing a lot of talking. Any minute now, I figured my interview would be next. I was next all right! The only thing on the TV screen was my back sitting on the mower driving up the pasture to the house. There went my TV career.

With Mom's enthusiasm about the mother-in-law apartment I felt compelled to ask her what would happen if she decided to move.

"Gene that will never happen"

But after one year she was homesick for her friends in Seattle and moved back to Bothell. I guess you should never say "never"

In February, 2000, I received a letter from someone I hadn't seen or thought I hadn't seen in thirty-four years. Surprise, surprise! It was from my high school sweetheart, Nancy, the dentist's daughter.

Dear Gene, just a few moments ago I was doing my Bible study lesson studying Romans. The question was asked "Who talked to you about the Gospel of Christ for the first time? My answer was Gene Olson. The next question was, have you thanked them? If not, what are you going to do about it?

Nancy continued writing a moving touching thank-you letter. I had never realized the impact my relationship had. How proud I had been to see Nancy at my church, standing at the podium singing "The Lord's prayer." Just a pretty little teenager with a magnificent voice from God. She had prayed at the altar. That was 1963.

I have continued to sing praised to Him throughout many lands—Singapore, Malaysia, Africa, Halti, Canada and across the U.S. This—all because you first told me how to know Jesus.

I knew Nancy had been singing in Churches. My brother had said he had heard her at a funeral. With all her recordings, I still haven't heard one song. Maybe someday.

The P.S. from Nancy, no response is necessary.

No response was necessary? I had to respond! I had to find out after all those years if she had actually walked in the flesh down the aisle to the Seattle VA psych ward or had it just been my hallucination.

I quickly sent a length letter thanking Nancy for her warm and tender words. I also wrote about the Navy South Vietnam and some experiences dealing with being bipolar. And at the end I asked please tell me Nancy was that you as a volunteer at the VA hospital in the early seventies?

She replied in part:

To answer your question about the VA Hospital in the early Seventies—yes that was me. After having two children I had wanted to have a day during the week where I could get out and do some volunteer work. A friend invited me to join a women's "guild" and volunteer there at the VA. I came to be a volunteer to the chaplain (Whitaker) and would often sing, minister or just write a letter for a patient. My favorite place in the hospital or, should I say, the plan where I felt the most needed, was the "psych" ward.

When I saw you walking toward me there, there was no question it was you. I stopped to talk to you and in utter dismay could not believe you would I be in a place in your life that would bring you to SUCH a valley. You looked dazed and haggard. I wasn't even sure you remembered me, or perhaps, I thought you were just so uncomfortable to have me see you there. At any rate, I run down to the chaplain's office. Thankfully he was there and not with anyone and I was able to sit and cry while I explained…it pained me to know little I knew about what was causing your pain. Now I know…

After Nancy's letter, there was a great sense of contemplation over my life. Before Lithium and after lithium. Twenty-seven years on twelve hundred milligrams of lithium kept me off the VA psych wards. safe, no problems, nothing to worry about.

But I felt I was just sitting on a fence, no emotionally deep feelings, observing world sailing by. To the bottom right, evil, hatred and sin swirled around. To the bottom left, goodness, love and peace shined bright. I was a good observer.

Sitting on the fence, I felt lithium was like a pop-up blocker, blocking all good or evil, and blocking out anything with emotions. I had nothing spiritual nothing emotional. In twenty-seven years I had cried once, when my father has died.

But there was a dilemma. Many times a tragic newspaper article would read: "He had a history of mental illness and went off his medication." I could not take chances. I had to stay on the fence with twelve hundred milligrams of Lithium as it destroys my thyroid gland, so I also took.0075 milligrams of Levoxyl. I don't recall when the goiter (enlargement of the thyroid gland) first started, it seemed to have always been there.

The first thyroid scan was in the eighties at Group Health Medical Ce Bellevue. I had had to lie down and slide my head in. Nothing was found.

During a physical in Indianapolis, the doctor called the resident.

"Come and look at this goiter. You don't see this very often."

It didn't bother me. Shirt collars hid it. Shaving was just sliding over a small hill, then in 2003, after all those years, my wife the doctor felt we should check extensively on the bulge of the thyroid gland.

I spent half a day at the Southwest Washington Medical Center having every type of scan known to the medical profession.

The doctor's reports: We can't find anything wrong.

This led my wife to seek out one of the best endocrinologists in Portland. More scans, more nothing.

The doctor wanted to do some biopsies. I had never had a biopsy before. It shouldn't be that bad. Ouch! Seven long wide needles penetrating the neck and thyroid gland! Seven! Seven in and seven out!

Report from the biopsy: I can't find anything wrong.

Besides the thyroid gland, since I had to consume large amounts of liquids with lithium, I was constantly going to the bathroom. I would drink something and in just several minutes I needed a bathroom. I knew at the restrooms in Vancouver and half the ones in Portland. And it was so frustrating travelling throughout Europe.

The Endocrinologists felt the prolonged used of lithium might be the problem. He suggested three choices: (1) Go completely off lithium (2) reduce the dosage of lithium or (3) find a more modern drug for bipolar disorder. Then more tests could be run and evaluated.

Going completely off lithium was not an option. After twenty-seven years the medicine was a good friend keeping me away from psych wards, but then too "normal of a lifestyle." I felt passive, unemotional.

Finding a more modern drug was too risky. To me that would be an automatic hospitalization.

Reducing the dosage of lithium was the only alternative. In the back of my mind How would I function at nine hundred (three capsules) six hundred two capsules), or three hundred (one capsule) milligrams? Would I be able to crawl off the fence of mediocrity?

Discussion with wife continued for several days. The fact that she was a medical doctor reinforced the decision to gradually reduce the lithium I would never have made the attempt without my wife's presence.

I was hoping my wife could have a lithium shot in reverse in case I started climbing the walls in a maniac high. No there was no such shot.

This time I was going to be more observant and more analytical to myself and surroundings to better understand bipolar. There was only one problem. All the other maniac episodes had happened in Seattle/Bothell and the Navy/South Vietnam. In the past twenty-seven years I had more experiences, travelled all over the United States and Europe. A surprise lay ahead.

The lithium reduction started. I could always feel mania approaching. Only a bipolar knows. For me, the fear advanced with the manic high. I didn't like it, I want it, but I could not stop it! Everything was unknown.

During the high, wow! You didn't want the mania to stop.

Standing on the front porch smoking my pipe, in my mind I saw Lucifer, author of confusion. In my silence, I yelled as loud as possible, "LUCIFER! BEHIND ME!" He disappeared like a little puppy dog with its tail between his legs. He was then peeking around the corner of my mind. I yelled again and I saw his face return.

This same period, I knew I would travel high and fast.

Still on the porch, I asked God to erase, delete, all bad memories, especially psych wards. I knew He could do it. I didn't want to relive the pain and agony in great detail as in other manias.

God's Spirit descended and answered, "I can't do it. If I erase your bad memories, I'll have to erase your good memories of love and happiness."

God knew I wouldn't go for that.

Then I saw the face of Jimmy Swaggart, when his hand was caught in the jar. He looked toward heaven, weeping, crying, begging for God's forgiven thousand tears rolled down the cheeks!

I told God I didn't want to be like Jimmy Swaggart. But when emotions s in my heart, all I wanted was just one tear. That's all I wanted, one tear. Inside the house, I knew soon I'd be flying high. I checked my wristwatch o'clock.

Now I was at the mouth of the Saigon River getting ready for Saigon. The water was muddy. Some shacks built on poles lined the river banks.

There was no liberty at Saigon; I could only see buildings.

On the way down the river the "Mekong Hilton" anchored in the Song Soirap River with Bravo and Charlie companies of the Ninth Infantry Division.

Standing watch, I saw the small boat approaching again. The green plastic tarp (body bag) and the only the same muddy boots reminded me of death.

Bouncing back to Vancouver the mania trip ended. With all the trains and country hopping I thought it had probably lasted three hours. I looked at my wrist watch 3:03. Three minutes! It was a fast "trip."

The lithium reduction continued. My wife was keeping track of the dosage and time intervals.

My younger son wanted a Kid's cuisine chicken nuggets TV dinner for lunch. I had fixed it many times. This time I could not concentrate. I stared at the TV dinner. I didn't Know where to start. I read the easy instructions. I couldn't get past step one. It was frustrating. My wife said, "That's OK, let me do it."

I answered, "No, I have to do it."

I couldn't do it.

I had to go the post office. Before I opened the door to the Windstar I glanced down. Was I wearing any pants? Did I have my shoes on?

As I was slowly driving down the roadway, a university choir started singing on the radio. Then a women's voice joined in. the choir sang from their hearts such perfect pitch and the woman's voice was also perfection. The climatic end jumped to the heavens.

The song was *Where He Leads Me I Will Follow*. I wanted to know who was singing. I waited impatiently for the announcer. There was silence. The music was overwhelming flooding my soul with tears.

"I thought we had a deal, God just one tear!"

The spirit of the Lord responded, "Look around. Do you see anyone in the van?"

"No."

"Then what are you worried about?"

"But God, I can't drive with tears blurring my vision!"

Instantly, I blinked. I could see perfectly.

I never found out who was singing.

Standing in line at the post office, the music played: I'm going to Kansas I'd never been to Kansas City, but it was the headquarters for the Church Nazarene. My mind switched to Nampa, Idaho, and some friends at Port Nazarene College. Then I heard "Twelfth Street and Vine." I'd never been to T Street and Vine, but I was at Hollywood and Vine during my honeymoon—so I was in Southern California for a while. Next in the song, I heard, "I might take a plane, been on many planes"; this time, I landed in Warsaw. "I might take a train"; push on a fast train swirling round and round in circles. I was speeding!

The song was interrupted with, "Hey, Mister! Can I help you over here?"

The bonus room was eight hundred square feet above the mother-in-law apartment. This was where I had my office, personal library, computer, printer, scanner and old trusty 1992 Smith Corona Personal Word Processor. All the walls were with twenty-six bookshelves, smaller ones beneath the windows.

My oldest son had placed two speakers on the wall in front of the sofa. I to compact discs out of the stereo. I wasn't sure if it was music or what, probably I replaced them with two of my favorites, classical and Abba.

On the classical CD the composer, orchestras and titles were all a mystery. Bach or Beethoven, maybe Mozart or Mendelssohn, perhaps it was a variety C there was no mystery to my love for the sounds, the incredible sounds filling my mind.

Switching to Abba, I got up and walked from the south window deck to the window, viewing the front pasture.

Abba started, "You can dance, you can dance. Having the time of your life

Laughter broke out as I saw myself sitting in the junior high school bleachers PE square dancing.

"Dancing is against my religion!"

I returned to classical, it was getting better and better. The volume increased higher.

I was back walking the same footsteps; I "kissed the teacher." I don't know who the teacher was, but she was kissed.

On the sofa again with classical.

Then Abba returned. "Thank you for the music." Music! What would life be without music?

"I believe in angels." I had to agree with Abba about believing in angels believed in angels. But the phrase "something good in everything I see." I was not sure if I could see good in everything.

The same day or next, I'm not sure, time was nonexistent but I had a visitor to the bonus room. Everyone was talking about Mel Gibson's The passion of the Christ, if it was a true portrayal according to Scripture, etc. Mel Gibson was my visitor to the bonus room, his spirit or my manic imagination.

Like Bud Abbott and Lou Costello with their comic Who's on first? Mel Gibson and I had a routine with Mount St. Helens.

We walked to the north window and there was Mount St. Helens in the pasture.

So close to the house you could peek right into the crater.

"Let's get out of here, it's going to blow!" Mel yelled.

"Mel, it's not going to blow."

Just then, a big puff of white steam and ash burst high.

"Gene, I know it's going to erupt."

"No Mel. Take it easy, it's not going to erupt."

"But look, the crater is getting bigger."

The bantering went on several more minutes until there was an explosion— not Mount St. Helens, but laughter between us.

Abbott and Costello would have been proud.

The 2004 presidential election had placed John Kerry in the spot light of Vietnam veterans. The slick video of a Swift boat was impressive on his website. As I read some articles on John Kerry the Song Soirap River caught by my eye. He had been on the same river a year after my ship was anchored as the Mekong Hilton.

John Kerry kept burning in my brain. Soon I was with him. I had an idea for a political rally.

Like at the mouth of Saigon River we started a small boat flotilla from the mouth of the Columbia River. Just before reaching the, I-5 Bridge we hugged the right side of Oregon. People were standing on the bridge waving flags and cheering.

Heading past the airport toward the gorge, we turned left toward Washington side Washougal Camas, Wintler Beach, past Vancouver and under the I-5 bridge again. Frenchman's Bar lay ahead where the flotilla stopped and John Kerry addressed the crown from his boat. The sandy beach was packed.

When it was over, John Kerry said, "That was a good idea, Gene. Is here anything I can do for you?"

I answered, "Yes, there is. I'd like a memorial for my friend Rich, a helicopter pilot killed in Vietnam."

A red, white and blue viewing stan was erected on top of the Seattle VA Medical Center, Beacon Hill.

Thousands of people had gathered on the hill and near the hospital for the memorial.

From the distant right, with the Cascade Mountains as a backdrop, a slow formation of helicopters appeared.

The first helicopter, the oldest military one in existence still flying, stops the viewing platform. We saluted the flag draped on its side. It continued flying over downtown Seattle and out Elliott Bay.

In progression, each helicopter became newer. Each helicopter stopped over Seattle and out Elliott Bay.

A helicopter like Rich's, a Huey, could barely fly to the viewing stand. The engine sputtered with smoke flying. The propellers flapped barely keeping it up. It took over Seattle and out Elliott Bay.

For the finale, hundreds of Blackhawks and the most modern helicopters stopped in formation at the viewing stand. The noise from the propellers was deaf Without warning, all the helicopters slowly descended over the crowd causing and scattering debris. People became afraid and ran.

Back in the bonus room, I wished what I saw and heard was true. But it wasn't.

Later I was thinking about a meeting I had had with my parents. The scene replayed in my mind. I was at the restaurant trying to explain to my parents the meaning of manic depression. I started from the beginning; by the middle. I knew they had no understanding. When I finished there was nothing else to say. I wanted them to know what I was experiencing. It was a big mistake.

I called my oldest sister, Aarlie on the telephone. As I told her about Mom and Dad to understand manic depression, but how I had failed to, a lump formed in my throat. I could not remember my last lump.

She said, "I think we should pray."

After hanging up, I told God I didn't think her prayer was very good. There was no enthusiasm, just a dull monotone voice.

The Spirit of the Lord said, "Your sister's prayer was a prayer of determination. And I heard it."

The lithium was decreasing by the hour. The confusion was increasing hour.

My wife, youngest son and I took a walk on the Columbia River. It was t time I compared the Columbia River to the Saigon River. There was no denying, the Columbia River was the most beautiful!

Almost to the van, I felt soon I'd lose all control of my thinking. The Spirit of God came.

"We are going to figure out this lithium. Soon it's going to be all over."

Tears came but not falling. If anyone saw tears, I'd blame it on my pipe smoke.

The next episode was not in the bonus room, but downstairs. I created a walking path from the TV room, to the kitchen, to the living room and back through the TV room. Before long I was back in Czestochowa, Poland. There was black Madonna, the most famous shrine of the Virgin in Poland. This was also the place where Pope John Paul II had made a pilgrimage back to his homeland. The platform was still standing. Once again, I stood where the Pope had stood, greeting millions of Poles. Now the field was empty. I imagined the people pressing toward for a closer look.

My sister – Aarlie's face appeared. Her head was tiled head she was smiling, laughing, so happy!

I silently said Well God we know what Aarlie's problem is. She won too many speech and debate tournaments in high school. And now she has all those trophies and all the answers.

A small vertical bar gauge appeared. There were no numbers on the side only a zero button at the bottom.

The gauge slowly started descending. As it descended, my mind was descending in confusion. My mind was entering a torment zone.

My sister Aarlie's face appeared again. Her head was tilted back smiling, laughing, so happy!

I wondered why!

The small vertical gauge was nearing zero, the bottom. My mind was spinning faster in confusion passed the tormented zone, beyond despair, into agony and suffering. I didn't know how much more I could possibly endure!

And my sister Aarlie's face appeared again. Her head was tilted back smiling, laughing, so happy!

Just before the vertical gauge fell to zero, I heard a voice. It sounded like the voice of God from the Columbia River before.

We are going to figure out this lithium. Soon it's going to be all over. But you can end all the confusion, agony and pain right now. It can be over now. All you have to do is take your own life.

Everything stopped. There was silent fear. Confusion ceased. No despair. No agony. No suffering. It was all replaced by fear. It was the greatest, most terrifying fear I had ever experienced. To think I was at the brink of committing suicide!

When my father had died, Mom had given me his old knives.

Where were my father's old butcher knives? Stay away from left hand cupboard.

On the counter was a large new bottle of lithium refill. That was what I needed more lithium! I was to swallow the whole bottle!

That would be stupid.

Thoughts focused on my family. How my death would affect them! My wife, the doctor, my Polish queen, had a heart of love overflowing! I could never hurt him!

My twelve-year old son, growing tall also, trying to figure out if he wanted to be a teenager. I could never hurt him!

Suicide hurts!

The final voice said, "I can't get you. But there are your boys. The author of confusion stopped. Putting on my pajamas in the master bath, I looked in the mirror.

"God, that was so close, so close!"

The Spirit of the Lord came. "I know. I was there. I saw everything. Now you know, why someone would commit suicide."

After all the years of trying to figure out why, why someone would want to kill themselves and all the times I had asked God to explain, He never had.

Instead of telling me, He had shown me. It was the Author of Confusion.

Lying in bed I concentrated on two things, sleeping and eating. If I could get a little sleep and eat something, maybe the lithium reduction wouldn't be so bad.

I couldn't sleep. Staring in the blackness, I knew if it wasn't for my wife next to me, I'd get up and walk to the Columbia River thinking it was the Saigon River.

The recollection is blurry on the start of my final episode. Standing on the small deck of the bonus room, I was softly crying. I don't know why. My seventeen-year- old son came, gently placed his big arms around me in a hug. We stood embraced. No one spoke.

Within hours, the lithium reduction would be over.

It was night. I had a plan for the Navy to have a rescue training exercise. It would take place in the back thirty acres. One helicopter would come in from the north, one from the south, one from the east and one from the west. As they were hovering over the pasture, the main helicopter would fly in over the cell tower light and land in the middle of the other helicopters. Several people would run to the house and rescue me.

The Navy never rescued me.

All memory went blank. My wife recalls the yelling and screaming about helicopters coming from the bonus room deck. My aggressive behavior scared her. She told me we should go to the hospital. I didn't think that was a good idea, but I went. My oldest son drove the van; the youngest was asleep in bed. It was so difficult for my wife to walk through the doors of the emergency room, doors she had walked through before as Dr. Olson

I remember nothing except when I was asked to go into a room, I saw a padded cell and refused.

My wife said I started screaming to everyone that I am a Vietnam Veteran.

The security guards arrived. I fought but was soon subdued to the floor.

Twenty-four hours later, I was knocked out with powerful Geodon, and the ambulance transferred me to Memorial Hospital Psych ward.

My wife's clinic was down the hall in the new wing addition of the hospital. She visited every morning but I was asleep.

Briefly, I awoke once. I quickly saw the face of my primary care physician; Dr. McDonald my wife's colleague then immediately fell asleep.

She told my wife I had asked who is going to drive the boys to school?

I awoke having to use the bathroom. There was an IV in my arm rolled the IV stand over to the toilet and had some trouble missing the dangling IV line

I had no memory.

Sounds were coming from the left I headed in that direction. It was a day room two or three people were there.

Back at the room a nurse came and removed the IV. Slowly short memories reappeared.

Within hours, my wife came and I was discharged. Five days of sleeping. This was the best psych ward I'd ever been on!

My wife felt the idea of lithium reduction had been a mistake. The mistake was going from twelve hundred milligrams to three hundred milligrams in fifteen days.

But there had been no way of knowing how everything would turn out. We had to try.

With the wife's observation and knowledge it was decided nine hundred milligrams three capsules was the proper dosage.

I told her we could probably have a lot of fun on six hundred milligrams, "Oh no, nine hundred milligrams!"

Daily I was asking God, why was the picture with my sister's head tilted back smiling, laughing? Why did it keep appearing as I walked through my agonizing tortured hell?

There was no answer for several days. I wanted to know.

Driving in the van with my wife to talk on the Columbia River I asked God again.

That picture of your sister was the happiest moment in her life.

My first reaction was Nobody knows... Oh yes God certainly knows.

One tear slowly rolled down the right side of my cheek and disappeared halfway. In my darkest gloom and misery, God had been showing the face of my sister in the happiest moment of her life.

I had to chuckle with God as I said, "Couldn't You have to put that tear on the left side of my face so my wife wouldn't see it?"

She saw nothing. She was busy planning our next trip to Poland. The only thing on her mind was Lublin.

At nine hundred milligrams, I was "off the fence"; feeling some emotions and able to tell the difference in dosage. It was amazing the difference one little capsule made.

My youngest boy said, "If Dad can just stay off the Saigon River, everything will be OK."

I replied, "Don't worry, Son, everything IS going to be OK."

In meditation with God, I said, "All these years I never wanted to die! All these years I have been fighting for my sanity!"

God answered, "I know. I was there. I saw it all. It was a good fight. And you won!"

# Epilogue

Psychiatry and pharmaceuticals research have moved fast from demon post-session to chemical imbalance of the brain.

Why can't psychiatrists balance the brain with their miracle drugs?

Wouldn't it be nice if we could balance brain like car tires are balanced but there is a great dilemma.

First, people must want help and second too many people finally get balance brains feel super great and then go off the medication because they feel well no longer in need

There is no death in this world so cruel, so sad, and so unexplained as suicide; it can be a mystery to all.

The National Alliance for the mentality ill in a 2 May 2001 news release stated:

*Every year, more than thirty thousand Americans take their own lives. Suicide is the eighth leading cause of death in the United States and third among our youth aged fifteen to twenty-four.*

*It's estimated 20 percent of people one in five suffering from bipolar disorder will kill themselves. And a staggering 50 percent of all people with this order will attempt suicide once in their lives.*

Oregon Senator Gordon Smith had a son with bipolar disorder who killed himself in his college apartment. Senator Smith said, "He was a beautiful boy and I loved him completely without completely understanding him."

On 8 July 2004, the Garret Lee Memorial Act passed the Senate. The bill was introduced by senator Gordon Smith who said it's been six months and it's time to find more meaning and help others who suffered like he did.

The bill is for suicide prevention.

I don't know what the boy from the boys' home was thinking. Later, as a young man, he hung himself.

264

I don't know what the veteran was thinking. His escape through the tiny Window screen at the VA hospital brought his death eight floors below.

I don't know what the young man was thinking. He tied his girlfriend to a chair and said "Now watch me die" as he hung himself.

I don't know what people think just before they kill themselves. If a note is left, may be, but at the exact moment of suicide the thinking is mystery.

I saw and heard the Author of Confusion. My wife with her medical knowledge does not believe in the author of confusion.

She has never met him. I pray she never will.

Years and years ago I recall asking a VA psychiatrist "Will I have to be on Lithium the rest of my life?"

His answer "You probably could try to go off. But it would be a gamble. Nobody knows."

Now I know.